CAT
FAMILY

SUDHANSHU THAKUR

BlueRose ONE .com
Stories Matter

First Published in July 2022

ISBN: 978-93-5628-857-7

BLUEROSE PUBLISHERS

www.BlueRoseONE.com

info@bluerosepublishers.com

+91 8882 898 898

Cover Design:

Muskan

Typographic Design:

Tanya Raj Upadhyay

Distributed by: BlueRose, Amazon, Flipkart

Contents

Contents

Contents

Contents

Bones , Muscles and Body of Lion

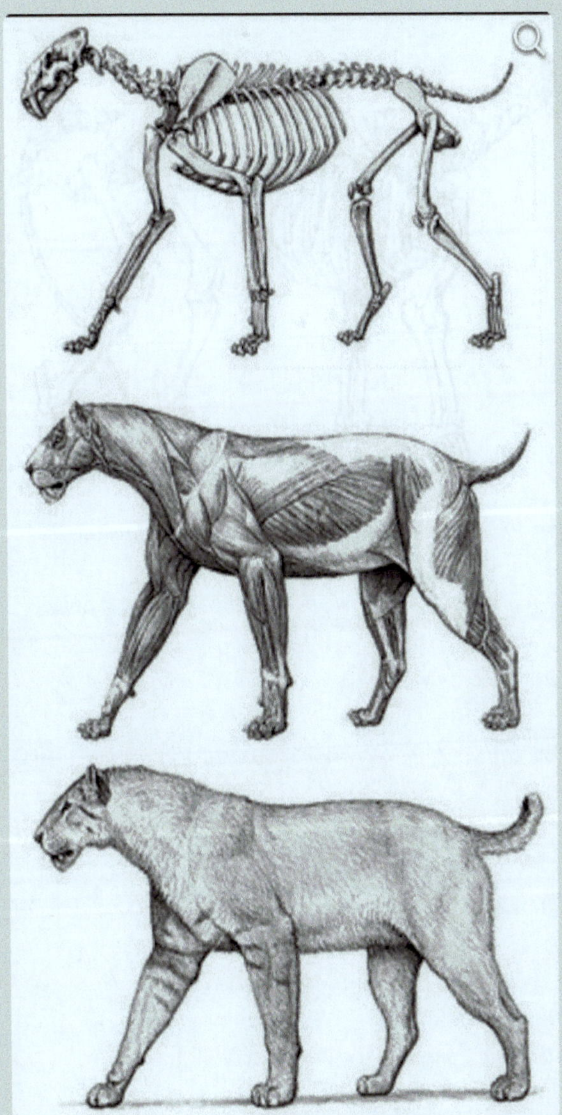

Structure of skeleton of lion

Lion's have 260 bones in their body.

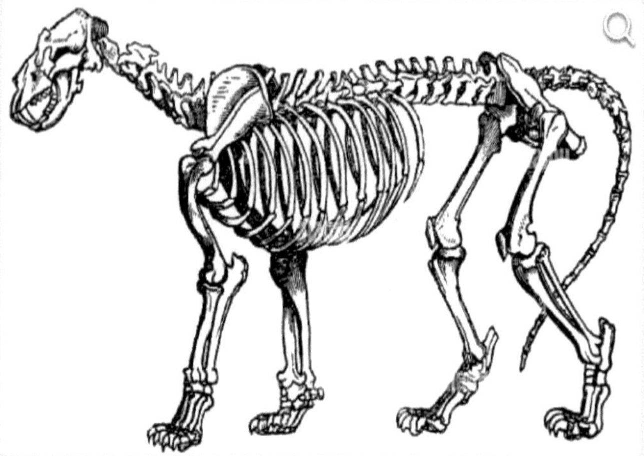

All cats species have 260 bones. The Bone in their forepaws are twisted in such a manner to give them the lion greater range of motion while running. The Lion's skull is very similar to a liger's but the distinct feature of lion's is the broader nose openings that are lower down on the skull then that of a liger's. They have a flexible spinal cord that consists of 30 spinal vertebrae. The skeleton system is extremely similar to that of a domestic cat. Skeleton are hard structures that help support and protect the body , and they can vary a lot.

Muscle of cat

बिल्ली की पेशी

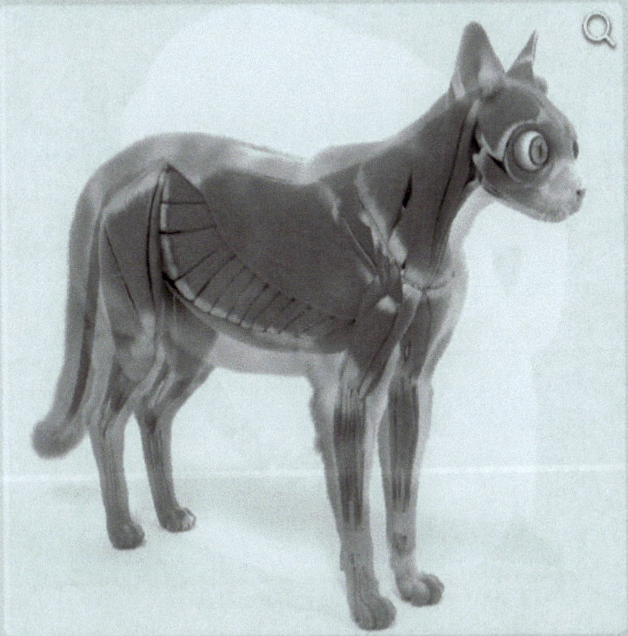

The two main integumentary muscles of a cat are the **platysma and the cutaneous maximus**. The cutaneous maximus covers the dorsal region of the cat and allows it to shake its skin. The platysma covers the neck and allows the cat to stretch the skin over the pectoralis major and deltoid muscles.

Skull of cat

बिल्ली की खोपड़ी

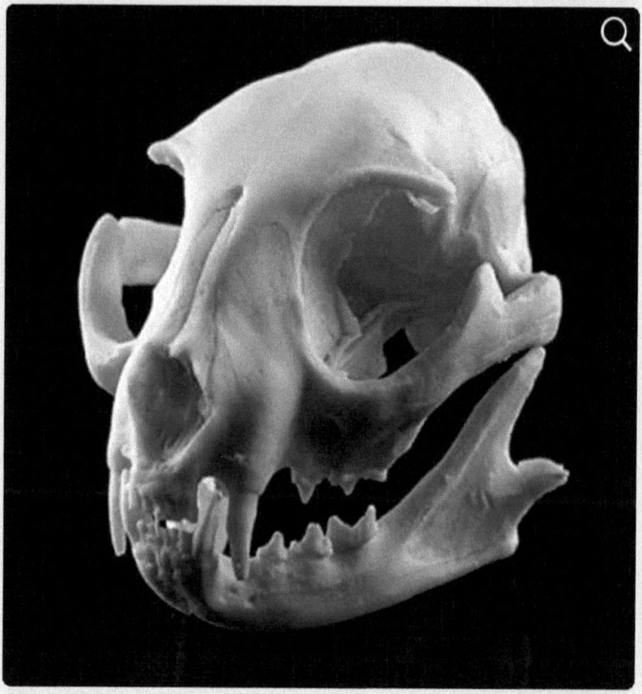

The cat skull is unusual among mammals in **having very large eye sockets and a powerful and specialized jaw**. Compared to other felines, domestic cats have narrowly spaced canine teeth, adapted to their preferred prey of small rodents.

Flexibility of cat

बिल्ली का लचीलापन

A cat's spine can rotate more than the spines of most other animals, and **their vertebrae** have a special, flexible, elastic cushioning on the disks, which gives it even more flexibility. ... Their shoulder blades are not attached with bone, but with muscle, and this gives a cat even greater extension and speed. Due to a cat's flexibility, **they can jump nine times their height**, and they will almost always land on their feet. Their spine and body structure allow them to brace for impact without getting hurt, for gentle and quiet landing.

Eyes of cat

बिल्ली की आंखें

The eyes of a cat are **protected** not only by the same types of eyelids that people have, but also by the nictitating membrane, which is sometimes called the third eyelid. This additional eyelid is a whitish pink color, and it is found under the other eyelids in the inside corner of the eye (near the nose). The eyes are placed face forward on the skull, in bony cavities called orbits. The white part of the eye is called the **sclera**, and it is covered with a thin membrane, the conjunctiva. The conjunctiva covers the inside of the eyelids.

Scientific classification of Lion

1. Kingdom. = Animalia

2. Phylum. = Chordata

3. Class. = Mammalia

4. Order. = Carnivora

5. Suborder. = Feliformia

6. Family. = Felidae

7. Sub family. = Pantherinae

8. Genus. = Panthera

9. Species. = P. Leo

10 Length. = 208 centimeters

11.Weight. = 190 kilograms

12.Speed. = 50 miles per hour

13 Lion are found in = Europe , Asia , Africa , Iran , Afghanistan , India.

Lion

Lion (शेर)

Lion are Carnivore animals. Lions may sleep 20 hours at day. Lions heels not touch to ground when he walk. Lions roars can heard as far as 5 miles away. Lions can run for short distances at 50 mph and lead as far as 36 feet. African lions are the most social of all big cats and they live together or "prides". A pride consist of about 15 lions. Lion is a special in the family Felidae and a member of the genus.

It has a muscular tuft at end of its tail.

Baby of Lion (Cubs)

Cubs (शावक)

Lion's babies stay with their mothers for about two years , by which stage they have joined the pride's hunting trip. After one to two years of nomadic life these young males drive out the resident males of a pride and take over the females. If a small group of males leave together they are able to hunt as a group and stand a better chance of being able to take over a pride. Females prefer their pride to have a large male coalition because it reduces the number of cubs lost to infanticide at take-overs.

Scientific classification of Tiger

1. Kingdom. = Animalia

2. Phylum. = Chordata

3. Class. = Mammalia

4. Order. = Carnivora

5. Suborder. = Feliformia

6. Family. = Felidae

7. Sub family. = Pantherinae

8. Genus. = Panthera

9. Species. = P. tigris

10. Length. = 390 centimeters

11. Weight. = 300 kilograms

12. Speed. = 40 miles per hour

13. Tiger are found in = India, Nepal, Bhutan, Russia, China, Asia, West Bengal, Siberia, Malaysia.

Tiger

Tiger (बाघ)

The **tiger** (*Panthera tigris*) is the largest living cat species and a member of the genus Panthera It is most recognisable for its dark vertical stripes on orange fur with a white underside. An apex predators , it primarily preys on unglates such as deer and wild boar. It is territorial and generally a solitary but social predator, requiring large contiguous areas of habitat which support its requirements for prey and rearing of its offspring. A tigers roar can heard as far as 3 kilometer. They are good swimmer.

Baby of Tiger (Cubs)

Cubs (शावक)

The saddest part is that Tiger cubs are born blind and only a few survive . Literally , the newborn cubs can't see anything , they only follow the scent of their mother. Since they are born blind and can't keep up , most of them die of hunger or cold. Some even get eaten by male Tigers to make the Tigress available for mating. That's just insane! When tiger cubs are born , they drink their mother's milk to survive. But when they have grown a little and are between 6 to 8 week old they can eat regular food , too.

Scientific classification of Lynx

1. Kingdom. = Animalia

2. Phylum. = Chordata

3. Class. = Mammalia

4. Order. = Carnivora

5. Suborder. = Feliformia

6. Family. = Felidae

7. Sub family. = Felinae

8. Genus. = Lynx

9. Species. = Felis Lynx

10. Length. = 130 centimeters

11. Weight. = 30 kilograms

12. Speed. = 50 miles per hour

13. Lynx are found in = America, Canada, Mexico, Europe, Asia, Russia, Himalayas, Australia, Italy, France.

Lynx

Lynx (वन बिलाव)

The lynx is a solitary cat that hunts the remote northern forests of North America , Europe and Asia. Lynx are covered with beautiful thick fur that keep them warm during frigid winters. Their large paws are also furry and hit the ground with a spreading toe motion that's make them function as natural snowshoes. These stealthy cats avoid humans and hunt at night , so they are rarely seen. There are several species of lynx. Few survival in Europe but that they do , like there Asian relatives , are typically larger than their North American counterpart , the Canada lynx.

Baby of Lynx (Kitten)

Kitten (बिलौटा)

Lynx are medium-sized cats that have a thick grayish-brown coat and short tail. They are easily identified by the pointed tufts of fur on their ears and cheeks. Their oversized paws act as snowshoes to prevent them form sinking in deep snow during the harsh winter of their native range which spans Alaska , Canada , and portions of the northern and western United States. Lynx have been known to give birth to up to 8 kittens in litter. However most litters have an average of 2 to 4 kitten.

Scientific classification of Clouded leopard

1. Kingdom.	=	Animalia
2. Phylum.	=	Chordata
3. Class.	=	Mammalia
4. Order.	=	Carnivora
5. Suborder.	=	Feliformia
6. Family.	=	Felidae
7. Sub family.	=	Pantherinae
8. Genus.	=	Neofelis
9. Species.	=	N. nebulosa
10. Length.	=	106 centimeters
11. Weight.	=	30 kilograms
12. Speed.	=	40 miles per hour

13. Clouded Leopard are found in = Himalayas , India , China , Nepal , Bhutan , Myanmar , Bangladesh , Thailand.

Clouded leopard

Clouded leopard (धूमिल तेंदुआ)

The clouded leopard is a medium-sized wild cat occurring from the Himalayas foothill through mainland Southern Asia into Southern China. Most cats are good climbers but the clouded leopard is near the top of its class. These cats can can even hang upside down beneath large branches , using their large paws and sharp claws to secure good grip. Clouded leopard have short , powerful legs equipped with rotation rear ankles that allow them to safely downclimb in a headfirst posture - much like a common squirrels.

Baby of Clouded leopard (Cubs)

Cubs (शावक)

Newborn clouded leopard cubs are very small and helpless , weighting only about 220-265 gram at birth. They are born with their closed eyes , no teeth , and unable to walk or move anywhere. Newborn clouded leopard lack the ability to control their body temperature very well , so special attention has to be given to keep the cubs warm. After the cubs are born , their keepers rub them briskly with the soft towel in order to clean them off , dry them , and simulate them. Then they are placed on soft blanket covering a heating pad in their nursery.

Scientific classification of Leopard

1. Kingdom.	=	Animalia
2. Phylum.	=	Chordata
3. Class.	=	Mammalia
4. Order.	=	Carnivora
5. Suborder.	=	Feliformia
6. Family.	=	Felidae
7. Sub family.	=	Pantherinae
8. Genus.	=	Panthera
9. Species.	=	P. pardus
10. Length.	=	190 centimeters
11. Weight.	=	60 kilograms
12. Speed.	=	36 miles per hour

13. Leopard are found in = Africa , Turkey , Asia , Himalayas , India , Russia , China , Sri Lanka.

Leopard

Leopard (तेंदुआ)

The leopard is one of the five extant species in the genus Panthera , a member of the Felidae. It occurs in a wide range in Sub-Saharan Africa , in small part of Western and Central-Asia.

On the Indian Subcontinent to Southeast and East Asia.

It can run at speed of up to 58 kilometers per hour. The earliest know as leopard fossils excavated in Europe are estimated 6,00,000 years old , dating to late Early Pleistocene.

It is similar in appearance to the jaguar but has a smaller , lighter physique , and its rosettes are generally smaller.

Baby of Leopard (Cubs)

Cubs (शावक)

Leopard cubs are relatively underdeveloped when born, due to the fairly short gestation period. For first three months of life, leopard consume nothing but mother's milk. They typically wean around three months of age after which time they share in the spoils of their mother's kill.

They stay with mom for approximately two years, during which they'll learn to hunt. Cubs are born with their closed eyes. When the eyes is open between 5 to 19 days after birth, the eyes appear blue due to lack of pigmentation.

Scientific classification of Black Panther

1. Kingdom. = Animalia

2. Phylum. = Chordata

3. Class. = Mammalia

4. Order. = Carnivora

5. Suborder. = Feliformia

6. Family. = Felidae

7. Sub family. = Pantherinae

8. Genus. = Panthera

9. Species. = Pardus

10. Length. = 76 centimeters

11. Weight. = 91 kilograms

12. Speed. = 50 miles per hour

13. Black Panther are found in = Asia , China , Burma , Nepal, India , Indonesia , Malaysia.

Black Panther

Black Panther (काला तेंदुआ)

Black Panther is the melanistic colour variant of any Panthera particular of the leopard (P. pardus) in Asia and Africa, and the jaguar (P. onca) in the America. Black Panther of both species have excess black pigments, but their typical spotted makings are also present. Melanism in the leopard is caused by a recessive allele, and jaguar by a dominant allele. Black Panther have good hearing, extremely good eyesight, and a strong jaw. The Black Panther is often called "the gost of the forest".

Baby of Black panther (Cubs)

Cubs (शावक)

After just 2-3 months, the cubs learn to hunt, and by the of age of 9 months they are able to bring down medium-sized prey.

Panthers cubs are not always born to panthers parents, however. The age of sexual maturity for the female panther is usually around two years, and she will have her first little at around 21/2 years old. The male panther is also capable of mating at age of two but, because of fierce competition for older males, does not usually have the opportunity until he is 3 or 4 years old. The one exception to this rule is during the mating season.

Scientific classification of Snow leopard

1. Kingdom.	=	Animalia
2. Phylum.	=	Chordata
3. Class.	=	Mammalia
4. Order.	=	Carnivora
5. Suborder.	=	Feliformia
6. Family.	=	Felidae
7. Sub family.	=	Pantherinae
8. Genus.	=	Panthera
9. Species.	=	P. uncia
10 Length.	=	115 centimeters
11.Weight.	=	32 kilograms
12.Speed.	=	40 miles per hour

13.Snow leopard are found in = Asia , Himalayas , China , Bhutan , Nepal , India , Pakistan , Afghanistan , Russia.

Snow leopard

Snow leopard (हिम तेंदुआ)

The snow leopard, also know as the ounce, is a large cat native to the mountains ranges of Central and Southern Asia. It is listed as Vulnerable on the ICUN Red list because of the global

population is estimated to number less than 10,000 mature individual and is expected to decline about 10% by 2040. They are insulated by thick hair-in shapes of gray or creamy yellow and covered with grayish black sport- and their wide, fur-covered feet act as natural snowshoes. These big cats can use their long tails for balance and as blankets to cover sensitive body parts against the several mountains chill.

Baby of Snow leopard (Cubs)

Cubs (शावक)

Snow leopard cubs are small and helpless when they are born , and do not open their eyes until they are about 7 days old At 2 months old , cubs are ready to eat solid food. For about 2 or 3 months , newborn cubs will remain in their well-protection den site , shielded away from predators. Their mother will stay close during that time , frequently returning to the den to nurse her cubs. Most likely , it's first taste of anything other than milk will be rare ibex or blue sheep that mom has brought home from a hunting trip.

Scientific classification of Bobcat

1. Kingdom.	=	Animalia
2. Phylum.	=	Chordata
3. Class.	=	Mammalia
4. Order.	=	Carnivora
5. Suborder.	=	Feliformia
6. Family.	=	Felidae
7. Sub family.	=	Felidae
8. Genus.	=	Lynx
9. Species.	=	L. Rufus
10. Length.	=	110 centimeters
11. Weight.	=	15.5 kilograms
12. Speed.	=	30 miles per hour

13. Bobcats are found in = Canada , America , Mexico , Africa , Europe , Asia , Spain.

Bobcat

Bobcat (छोटा वनबिल)

These medium-sized cats are similar to their cousin , the lynx , but a bit smaller. At 11 to 30 pounds , they are roughly twice the size of a housecat. Through their bobbed tails are shorter at only 4 to 7 inches. Although they are very adaptable and live in diverse habitats like forests, swamps , deserts , and even suburban areas , they are elusive and nocturnal and thus not seen very often. While bobcat populations in many areas plummeted during the early 20th century because of the popularity of their fur , international laws now protect them and their numbers have rebounded significantly.

Baby of Bobcat (kitten)

Kitten (बिलौटा)

Bobcats have a litter size of about 1-6 kitten's. The kitten are born blind and cannot open their eyes until around 10 days have passed. At first these kittens will survive only on their mother's milk. Kitten will begin eating solid food at around 2 months. By 5 months these kitten will begin learning how to hunt. Somewhere between , 8 to 11 months , kitten will be ready to leave their mother's den and begin becoming more independent. They start preparing for adulthood immediately in life.

Scientific classification of Cheetah

1. Kingdom.	=	Animalia
2. Phylum.	=	Chordata
3. Class.	=	Mammalia
4. Order.	=	Carnivora
5. Suborder.	=	Feliformia
6. Family.	=	Felidae
7. Sub family.	=	Feliformia
8. Genus.	=	Acinonyx
9. Species.	=	A. jubatus
10. Length.	=	94 centimeters
11. Weight.	=	72 kilograms
12. Speed.	=	80 miles per hour

13. Cheetahs are found in = Africa , Iran , Angola , Botswana , Namibia , Zambia , Asia , Sahara.

Cheetah

Cheetah (चीता)

The cheetah is the fastest land animal in the world. They can reach a top speed of around 130 kilometers per hour. A cheetah can accelerate from 0 to 130 kilometers in just few seconds. Cheetahs are extremely fast however they tire quickly and can only keep up their top speed for a few minutes before they are too tired to continue. Cheetahs are smaller than other members of the big cat family , weighting only 45-60 kilogram. One way to always recognise a cheetah is by the long , black lines which run from the inside of each eye to the mouth.

Baby of Cheetah (Cubs)

Cubs (शावक)

Baby of cheetahs are called cubs and are usually born in litters of 3-5 They are blind at birth and are covered with a thick coat of fur, called a mantle, which helps to protect them from predators. In the wild, cheetahs cubs have a high mortality rate, approximately 90%, and it is estimated that 50 to 75% of cheetah cub die before they reach 3 months of age. The mantle is shed gradually during the first year and a half of a cheetah's life as the cub grows and learns to be an independent hunter and adult.

Scientific classification of Mountain Lion

1. Kingdom.	=	Animalia
2. Phylum.	=	Chordata
3. Class.	=	Mammalia
4. Order.	=	Carnivora
5. Suborder.	=	Feliformia
6. Family.	=	Felidae
7. Sub family.	=	Felinae
8. Genus.	=	Puma
9. Species.	=	P. concolor
10.Length.	=	227 centimeters
11.Weight.	=	100 kilograms
12.Speed.	=	50 miles per hour

13 Puma are found in = Europe , Turkey , America , Canada , Florida , Mexico , Alaska , Patagonia , California.

Mountain Lion

Mountain Lion (पहाड़ी शेर)

The Mountain Lion is a remarkable creature of the wild. The Mountain Lion is top predator and the largest wild cat of the America. Female mountain lions weigh slightly less than males. The colour of adults Mountain Lion is tawny. Mountain Lion are capable of running at speed of up to 45 miles per hour. Mountain Lion are skilled climbers , frequently dwelling in trees. Mountain Lion are a generalist predator - it will eat any animal it can catch , from insects to large animals like elk , moose , deer and bighorn sheep.

Baby of Mountain Lion (Cubs)

Cubs (शावक)

Cubs are born with their closed eyes. When the eyes open between 5 and 19 days after birth. the eyes appear blue due to lack of pigmentation. At approximately 5 months of age. The cubs eyes turn brown and remain brown throughout the their life. Adult Lion are brown. tawny gray or red in colour. However , when the cubs is born, the fur is brown with black spots on the body and bars on the tail. When the cubs reaches 2 months of age , the spots being to fade and the cub starts to grow into its adult coloring.

Scientific classification of Jaguar

1. Kingdom. = Animalia

2. Phylum. = Chordata

3. Class. = Mammalia

4. Order. = Carnivora

5. Suborder. = Feliformia

6. Family. = Felidae

7. Sub family. = Pantherinae

8. Genus. = Panthera

9. Species. = Panthera onca

10. Length. = 200 centimeters

11. Weight. = 96 kilograms

12. Speed. = 50 miles per hour

13. Puma are found in = America , Mexico , India , Canada , China , Asia , Argentina , Brazil.

Jaguar

Jaguar (जैगुआर)

The jaguar panthera onca is the largest cat in the Americas and the third-largest cat in the world after tigers and lions. They look lot like leopards. They have mighty name. The word "jaguar", which means' he who kills with one leap'. Their territory is shrinking. They're on the chunky side. They've got spotty spots. Jaguar are excellent swimmer. The jaguar is a large feline species and the only extant member of the genus Panthera native to the Americas. Both males and females roar , which helps bring them together when the want to mate.

Baby of Jaguar (cubs)

Cubs (शावक)

They are born with their eyelids sealed shut. After about 2 week , the cubs are able to see for first time. After 6 months , the cubs mother will teach them to hunt , and after their second birthday , the cubs will leave their mother to live on their own. The mortality rate for baby jaguar is very high , and many are eaten by large anaconda snakes that also live in the rain forest and jungles. After the first two years of their life with their mothers and siblings , jaguars will go off on their own to find their own hunting territories.

Scientific classification of Cougar

1. Kingdom. = Animalia

2. Phylum. = Chordata

3. Class. = Mammalia

4. Order. = Carnivora

5. Suborder. = Feliformia

6. Family. = Felidae

7. Sub family. = Felinae

8. Genus. = Puma

9. Species. = Felis concolor

10. Length. = 240 centimeters

11. Weight. = 82 kilograms

12. Speed. = 50 miles per hour

13. Puma are found in = America , Florida , Canada , Columbia , Asia , Australia , Africa.

Cougar

Cougar (कुठर)

The cougar , which is also commonly referred to as a puma , mountain lion or panther , is the second largest cat in North America. Unlike other big cats , however , the cougar cannot roar. Instead , the large feline purrs like a house cat. Cougar also have similar body types to house cats , only one a large scale. They have slender bodies and round head with pointed ears. They vary between 1.5-2.7 m from head to tail. While males can weigh up to 68 kg , females weigh less , topping out at nearly 45 kg.

Baby of Cougar (kitten)

Kitten (बिलौटा)

Baby of cougar's are called kittens and remain with their mother for up to the first two years of their lives. Female give birth to little averaging between one and six cubs after only three months of gestation. According to the cougar fund, female cougar spend approximately three-quarters of their lives pregnant or rising cubs. When the cubs is born, the fur is brown with black spots on the body and on the tail. When the cubs reaches 2 months of age, the spots being to fade and the cub starts to grow into its adult coloring.

Scientific classification of Golden cat

1. Kingdom. = Animalia

2. Phylum. = Chordata

3. Class. = Mammalia

4. Order. = Carnivora

5. Suborder. = Feliformia

6. Family. = Felidae

7. Sub family. = Felinae

8. Genus. = Caracal

9. Species. = Caracal Aurata

10. Length. = 101 centimeters

11. Weight. = 16 kilograms

12. Golden cat are found in = Asia, Nepal, Indonesia, Bhutan, China, America, Africa, Bangladesh.

Golden cat

Golden cat (सुनहरी बल्ली)

The Asians golden cat is a medium-sized wild cat native to the northeastern India subcontinent. Southwest Asia, and southern China. The African golden cat remain little know by science. through within Africa there is much tribal superstition about it. It is also called the 'leopard's' brother, according to the local people it follows the leopard. The colour of its fur ranges from sepia-gray to marmalade orange-red, and it sometimes has spots , and could be spotted all over.

Baby of Golden cat (Kitten)

Kitten (बिलौटा)

Golden cat is solitary creature most of its lifetime, except during the mating season. Pregnancy in females lasts 75-78 days and ends with one or two kitten's. Mother give birth in well hidden den, usually in hollow tree. Kittens have only 6.3 to 8.3 ounces at birth, but they grow and develop quickly. Golden cat's kittens are blind at birth and are covered with same colour fur as adult cats. They open their eyes in 6 to 12 days after being born. Golden cats communicate with meowing, hissing, purring and growling.

Scientific classification of Fishing cat

1. Kingdom. = Animalia

2. Phylum. = Chordata

3. Class. = Mammalia

4. Order. = Carnivora

5. Suborder. = Feliformia

6. Family. = Felidae

7. Sub family. = Felinae

8. Genus. = Prionailurus

9. Species. = Prionailurus Viverrinus

10 Length. = 78 centimeters

11.Weight. = 16 kilograms

12.Speed. = 34 miles per hour

13.Fishing cat are found in = Southeastern Asia , Sri Lanka , Pakistan , India , Southern China , Java , Sumatra , Nepal , Bangladesh , Cambodia , Myanmar , Thailand .

Fishing cat

Fishing cat (मचछवारा)

The fishing is a solitary and nocturnal hunter that rests during the day amongst dense vegetation an then at night heads to the water to find food. They are extremely strong and able swimmers and can swim huge distances , often while pursuing a fish. These animal's are largely territorial and occupy home ranges as large as 22 sq. km. Fishing cats are able to kill large prey such as dogs , civets and domestic cattle. Fishing cat has interesting fishing techniques. It gently touches the water with its paws to produce miniature waves like insects that are landing on the surface of water. This attracts fish.

Baby of Fishing cat (Kitten)

Kitten (बिलौटा)

After a gestation of 63 days, females produce 1-4 young are suckled to the age of six months and become independence once they are ten months old. In the wild, fishing cats live up to an age of 12 years on an average.They weigh 3. 5-6 ounces at birth and will gain and average of 11 grams per day. Their eyes open by the 16 th day, and meat is usually taken around the 53 rd day. They are weaned between 4-6 months of age, reach adult size around 8-9 months old and are independent around 10 months. There male season is Jan to Feb.

Scientific classification of Caracal

1. Kingdom. = Animalia

2. Phylum. = Chordata

3. Class. = Mammalia

4. Order. = Carnivora

5. Suborder. = Feliformia

6. Family. = Felidae

7. Sub family. = Felinae

8. Genus. = Caracal

9. Species. = Caracal Aurata

10. Length. = 74 centimeters

11. Weight. = 12 kilograms

12. Speed. = 50 miles per hour

13. Caracal are found in = Saharan Africa , Tropical rainforest , Africa , Asia , India.

Caracal

Caracal (करकाल)

The caracal is a medium-sized wild cat native to Africa, The Middle East, Central Asia, and India. It is characterized by a robust build, long legs, a short face, long tufted ears, and long canine teeth. It's coat is uniformly reddish tan or sandy, while the ventral parts are lighter with small reddish marking. It reaches 40-50 cm (16-20 in) at the shoulder and weighs 8-19 kg (18-42 lb). It was first scientifically describe by German naturalist Johann Christian Daniel von Schreber in 1776. The caracal is also know as the Persian lynx and the gazelle cat.

Baby of Caracal (Kitten)

Kitten (बिलौटा)

After a gestation of approximately 78-81 days , female produce a letter of 1-4 kittens , with 2 being the average. They being to open their eyes on their first day of life , but it takes 6-10 days for them to completely open. They are weaned at 10 weeks , and will remain with their mothers for up to a year. They attain sexual maturity between 12-16 months. In captivity , Caracals have lived up to 19 years. Unlike the other small African cats , Caracals will not hesitate to kill prey larger than themselves , such as adult springbok or young Kudu. They born with their closed eyes.

Scientific classification of White panther

1. Kingdom. = Anamalia

2. Phylum. = Chordata

3. Class. = Mammalia

4. Order. = Carnivora

5. Suborder. = Feliformia

6. Family. = Felidae

7. Sub family. = Felinae

8. Genus. = Caracal

9. Species. = Caracal Aurata

10. Length. = 74 centimeters

11. Weight. = 72 kilograms

12. Speed. = 50 miles per hour

13. Caracal are found in = Tropical rainforest, Africa, Asia, Saharan Africa, Montane forest, Evergreen rainforest.

White panther

White panther (सफेद तेंदुआ)

The reason that this mutation is so rare is that it is huge disadvantage for the cat. A "White Panther" cannot camouflage itself when it is hunting. This makes it much harder for this type of cat to catch it's prey , which usually leads to starvation. This is not true for a "black panther". White Panther are know to be one of the rarest animals breed in the world. A white panther is a white specimen of any of several species of larger cat. White Panthers may be the result of albinism , leucism or the chinchilla mutation.

Baby of White panther (Cubs)

Cubs (शावक)

Typically , a panther litter consists of two to three cubs but , sometimes , up to six. Panthers cubs are born with their eyes closed and are covered with faintly white fur. They weight about 450 to 1000 g (16 to 35 oz). The mother has to stay at the den all the time during the first few days after the birth to rest and nurse the newborn cubs. Meanwhile cubs spend most of their time sleeping and nursing on their glazed eyes and get their first glimpse of the world. While the cubs still lack of mobility , the mother have to leave her cubs unattended as she travels far form the birth den to find food for her family.

Scientific classification of Cretan wild cat

1. Kingdom. = Animalia

2. Phylum. = Chordata

3. Class. = Mammalia

4. Order. = Carnivora

5. Suborder. = Feliformia

6. Family. = Felidae

7. Sub family. = Felinae

8. Genus. = Felis

9. Species. = F. silvestris

10. Length. = 50 centimeters

11. Weight. = 8 kilograms

12. Speed. = 50.0203 miles per hour

13. Cretan wild cat are found in = Europe, Greek island, Africa.

Cretan wild cat

Cretan wild cat (क्रेटन जंगली बील्ली)

The body of the Cretan wild cat is larger than ordinary cats. The males reach a body length of 50 cm and a tail length of 30 cm. The tail is narrower on its base and more bushy at its end. Moreover, the coat color is light brown with dark spots and streaks. The tail has several black rings and it's end is always black. The cats feed on rabbits, birds, insects, and rodents, while they live in Rocky areas and isolated forests at an altitude of 900-1200m. The Cretan wild cat is a member of the genus Felis that inhabits the Greek island of Crete. It's taxonomic status is unclear at present.

Baby of Cretan wild cat (Kitten)

Kitten (बिलौटा)

They bear 4-7 kittens , once or twice a year. Females are pregnant for 56 to 68 days and give birth to 1 to 8 young , with an average of 3.4 , in a protected burrow , often a space under rocks or in dense vegetation. Females become sexually mature at about 10 to 11 months old , and males form 9 to 22 months old. Birth occur usually in May. The young is classified as being as "kitten" from birth up until roughly 1 year in age. Most around 5 to 6 months , although it varies greatly. Some cats hit puberty as young as 4 months , while it can take over a year for other.

Scientific classification of Feral cat

1. Kingdom. = Animalia

2. Phylum. = Chordata

3. Class. = Mammalia

4. Order. = Carnivora

5. Suborder. = Feliformia

6. Family. = Felidae

7. Sub family. = Felinae

8. Genus. = Felis

9. Species. = F. catus

10. Length. = 46 centimeters

11. Weight. = 4.5 kilograms

12. Speed. = 30 miles per hour

13. Feral cat are found in = Australia , Rome , Europe , Persia , Siamese , Africa.

Feral cat

Feral cat (जंगली बील्ली)

Feral cats are domestic cats that were born and raised with little or no contact with people. Feral cats often live in colonies , forming groups around food sources. Killing feral cats does not lower their numbers. New feral cats will soon take up their place. If you feed feral cats , you have to TNR , to prevent overpopulation. Feral cats are just as healthy as pet cats. Feral cats thrive in all landscapes- form the most rural to the inner city Feral cats are domestic cats-the same species as pet cats. Unlike pet cats , they are unadoptable. Feral cats are not stray cats. Strays are homeless pet cats.

Baby of Feral cat (Kitten)

Kitten (बिलौटा)

Feral moms usually give birth in quite, unseen spots where kittens will not be visible for several weeks. Older kittens can also be captured and tamed but the process gets slower and less successful the longer the kittens stay in the wild. The process of taming kittens can take form 2 to 6 weeks (longer for some exceptionally skittish kittens) depending on their age and state of wildness. A kitten may hiss and "spit" at humans. They are usually terrified of humans. The kitten which acts the most ferocious is just the most scared, but it is capable of giving you a nasty scratch or bite and will probably try to escape if given the change.

Scientific classification of European Wild cat

1. Kingdom. = Animalia

2. Phylum. = Chordata

3. Class. = Mammalia

4. Order. = Carnivora

5. Suborder. = Feliformia

6. Family. = Felidae

7. Sub family. = Felinae

8. Genus. = Felis

9. Species. = F. silvestris

10. Length. = 65 centimeters

11. Weight. = 7 . 5 kilograms

12. Speed. = 30 miles per hour

13. European Wild cat are found in = Europe , Scotland , Turkey , Caucasus , Iberian Peninsula , Italy , England , Wales , Germany.

European Wild cat (यूरोपीयन जंगली बील्ली)

The European Wild cat Felis Silvesteris is the size of a large domestic cat. It has a broad head and wide set ears. Their coat is thick and long in winter, grey-brown with a well-defined, individual patten of black stripes on the head, neck, limbs, and a distinct dorsal line. It has a bushy, blunt-ending tail with several black rings and a black tip. Some individuals have a white spot on the throat.

In the winter coat, this wild cat looks rather compact and short-legged, although in reality they have longer legs than most domestic cat.

Baby of European Wild cat (Kitten)

Kitten (बिलौटा)

The mating season is in late winter : January-March.

Most births take place in April and May. The estrus cycle lasts for 1-6 days when males are present and the gestation for 64-71 days , on average 68 days. Age at independence can vary from 5-10 months and sexual maturity is reached by females at 6. 5-11 months and for males at 9-10 months. Kittens starts to eat solid food when they are one month old , are weaned at the age of 3. 5-4. 5 months , and lean to hunt progressively between 3-5 months of age. Longevity is 12-16 years of age.

Scientific classification of Arabian Wild cat

1. Kingdom. = Animalia
2. Phylum. = Chordata
3. Class. = Mammalia
4. Order. = Carnivora
5. Suborder. = Feliformia
6. Family. = Felidae
7. Sub family. = Felinae
8. Genus. = Felis
9. Species. = F. lybica
10. Length. = 65 centimeters
11. Weight. = 8.165 kilograms
12. Speed. = 30 miles per hour
13. Arabian Wild cat are found in = Arabia.

Arabian Wild cat

Arabian Wild cat (अरबियन जंगली बील्ली)

The cat's ferocity is well noted by tribesmen, who say, "they would rather tackle a wild leopard than a Gordon's [Arabian] wildcat." The Arabian Wild cat may be some what protected in Islamic society because the Prophet Mohammed is said to have loved them. The Arabian Wild cat (Felis lybica lybica), also called Gordon's wild cat is a wild cat subspecies that inhabits the Arabian Peninsula. It was first described in 1968 by British zoologist David Harrison who named it Felis silvestris gordoni in honour of Major A. C. Gordon who collected the type specimen in Oman.

Baby of Arabian wild cat (Kitten)

Kitten (बिलौटा)

Kittens have an incredibly rapid period of growth and development in their first few weeks of life. They are born with the eyes and ears closed. They cannot walk but they crawl on their tummies and rely on their developing sense of smell to find Mum and feed from them.

By 2 weeks of age, the kitten's eyes have opened.

By 3 weeks of age, the kitten's ear canal has fully opened.

By 4 weeks of age, the kitten can eliminate urine and faeces on their own, before this, they rely on the mum to stimulate them to excrete their waste.

Scientific classification of Asiatic Wild cat

1. Kingdom.	=	Animalia
2. Phylum.	=	Chordata
3. Class.	=	Mammalia
4. Order.	=	Carnivora
5. Suborder.	=	Feliformia
6. Family.	=	Felidae
7. Sub family.	=	Felinae
8. Genus.	=	Felis
9. Species.	=	F. lybica
10. Length.	=	64 centimeters
11. Weight.	=	7. 7 kilograms
12. Speed.	=	30 miles per hour

13. Asiatic Wild cat are found in = Asia , China , India .

Asiatic Wild cat

Asiatic Wild cat (एशियाई जंगली बील्ली)

The Asiatic Wild cat has light colored fur with spots on its upper body. It is smaller than the European Wild cat with lighter fur. The cat's tail is long , thin and tapering with a black rings and a black tip. There are very few spots on the cat's lower throat and neck. Asian Wild cats also have a dark stripe from the corner of its eye to the base of its ear , and tufts of hear above its ears. The cat's legs ate longer than the legs of a domestic cat. You can find Asiatic cat in the lower desert and semi-desert areas near the Caspian sea. They also inhabit Iran , Afganistan , India and China.

Baby of Asiatic Wild cat (Cubs)

Kitten (शावक)

The mating season various depending on the region. Litters generally range in size from 2 to 4 cubs. Female wildcats will often mate with male domestic cats. Asiatic wildcats live up to 11 years.

Their breeding season varies depending on climate conditions and after a gestation period of 60 - 70 days , 2 to 4 kittens are born.

They stay less than a year before they separate from their mother.

Sexual maturity is reached by 13 to 14 months. During the mating season , males fight viciously , and may congregate around a single female.

Scientific classification of African Wild cat

1. Kingdom. = Animalia
2. Phylum. = Chordata
3. Class. = Mammalia
4. Order. = Carnivora
5. Suborder. = Feliformia
6. Family. = Felidae
7. Sub family. = Felinae
8. Genus. = Felis
9. Species. = F. lybica
10. Length. = 70 centimeters
11. Weight. = 4.5 kilograms
12. Speed. = 57.166 miles per hour
13. African Wild cat are found in = Asia , Africa.

African Wild cat

African Wild cat (अफ्रीका का जंगली बील्ली)

The African Wildcat is also know as the Desert Cat, African Desert Cat or simply Wildcat. The African Wildcat is widespread in Africa and its range extends into the Middle East. The African Wildcat looks similar to a short-haired domestic tabby cat, but has reddish colouring on the back of the ears, over its abdomen and on the back of its hind legs. African Wildcats diverged from the other Wildcat subspecies about 131,000 years ago. Some individuals were first domesticated about 10,000 years ago in the Middle East.

Baby of African Wild cat (Kitten)

Kitten (बिलौटा)

Like domestic cats, African wildcats breed throughout the year, but the timing varies among regions. After a 56- to 65-day pregnancy, the **female gives birth to between one and five kittens** in a protected den. Females use burrows abandoned by other species for birthing and raising their young. African wild cats occur throughout Africa in a wide variety of habitats. They are absent only from tropical rainforest.

Scientific classification of Serval cat

1. Kingdom. = Animalia

2. Phylum. = Chordata

3. Class. = Mammalia

4. Order. = Carnivora

5. Suborder. = Feliformia

6. Family. = Felidae

7. Sub family. = Felinae

8. Genus. = Leptailurus

9. Species. = L. serval

10. Length. = 83 centimeters

11. Weight. = 12 kilograms

12. Speed. = 49.71 miles per hour

13. Serval cat are found in = Africa, Sahara, Sahel,

Savannah.

Serval cat

Serval cat (सर्वल बिल्ली)

Servals have long , powerful legs that are important for jumping. They have been know to jump as high as 3.6 m (12 ft) to catch birds in mid air. Servals' large ears act as radar dishes to locate food. These cats listen for the movement of animals in the grass before they pounce. It is believed that they use their ears as much as their eyes. They like most cats , live a solitary existence. Servals are leggy. Servals communicate with pee. Both males and females mark their territories by spraying urine on trees and bushes , scraping fresh urine in the ground with their claws.

Baby of Serval cat (Kitten)

Kitten (बिलौटा)

Servals are solitary animals except when breeding.

They are polygynous , and the territories of males overlap with those of as many females as possible for optimal reproduction. Although there is no set breeding interval , mating occurs more often in the spring.

A female nearly ready to breed will hunt and court the male over several days , just before coming into oestrus. After a gestation period of 10 - 11 weeks , female servals give birth to 2-3 kittens.

These young , about 250g at birth , double in size in their first 11 days. Males take 1-2years to establish a new territory.

Scientific classification of Ocelot cat

1. Kingdom. = Animalia

2. Phylum. = Chordata

3. Class. = Mammalia

4. Order. = Carnivora

5. Suborder. = Feliformia

6. Family. = Felidae

7. Sub family. = Felinae

8. Genus. = Leopardus

9. Species. = L. pardalalis

10. Length. = 100 centimeters

11. Weight. = 20 kilograms

12. Speed. = 38 miles per hour

13. Ocelot cat are found in = America , Mexico , Arizona , Texas , Lowland , Brazil .

Ocelot cat

Ocelot cat (ओसेलॉट बिल्ली)

The Ocelot or dwarf leopard is found in every South American country apart form Chile and as far north as Mexico and Texas. This is mainly in or around tropical forest , thorn forest , mangrove swamps and savanna. They are meat eaters and like to eat all sorts , including deer , snakes , fish , bird , rabbits and rodents... they're not fussy! Ocelots are nocturnal and usually hunt at night but they have been know to hunt as early as dusk or as late as dawn. The color of an ocelot ranges form a very light yellow to a dark reddish-grey , but all have dark spots and strips.

Baby of Ocelot cat (Kitten)

Kitten (बिलौटा)

Baby ocelots are called kittens. Kittens are very small at birth, weighing only 7 to 12 ounces (200 to 340 grams). Born with sealed eyes, kittens gain their first glimpse of their mother at 14 days old. Male and Female mate between 5 and 10 times daily during mating season. They must mate so many times because it is very hard to get a female ocelot pregnant. Kittens may live in their mother's territory for up to two years before setting off on their own. They live to around 13 years, on average.

Scientific classification of Pallas cat

1. Kingdom. = Animalia

2. Phylum. = Chordata

3. Class. = Mammalia

4. Order. = Carnivora

5. Suborder. = Feliformia

6. Family. = Felidae

7. Sub family. = Felinae

8. Genus. = Otocolobus

9. Species. = O. manul

10.Length. = 57 centimeters

11.Weight. = 3 kilograms

12.Speed. = 30 miles per hour

13.Pallas cat are found in = Asia, Iran, China, India.

Pallas cat

Pallas cat (पलास बिल्ली)

Palla's cats appear to be bigger and heavier than they actually are due to their stocky builds and long , dense coats. Unlike other cats , the pupils of Pallas ' cats contract into small circles rather than vertical slits. Their fur is nearby twice as long on their belly and tail as on their top and sides. Presumably , this helps keep the cats warm as they hunt on snow or frozen ground. Within this range , Pallas cats prefer the cold and arid enviroments of rocky steppes and grasslands at elevations up to about 15,000 feet. The Pallas' cats compact body makes it a poor runner.

Baby of Pallas cat (Kitten)

Kitten (बिलौटा)

They have an extremely short mating season. Female Pallas' cats are in estrus for only 26 to 42 hours , a shorter period than most cats. Mating occurs in February and March and females give birth to a litter of two to six kittens in April and May. By four months old , the kittens being hunting with their months , They're ready to breed at the age of ten to eleven months. Pallas ' cats (Otocolobus manul) have a pronounced reproductive seasonality controlled by photoperiod. Although mating attempts during this study were unsuccessful.

Scientific classification of Sand cat

1. Kingdom. = Animalia

2. Phylum. = Chordata

3. Class. = Mammalia

4. Order. = Carnivora

5. Suborder. = Feliformia

6. Family. = Felidae

7. Sub family. = Felinae

8. Genus. = Felis

9. Species. = F. margarita

10 Length. = 51 centimeters

11.Weight. = 2. 8 kilograms

12.Speed. = 24. 85 miles per hour

13.Sand cat are found in = Africa , Sahara , Algeria , Niger , Morocco , Arabian Peninsula , Asia , Turkmenistan , Iran , Pakistan , Afghanistan .

Sand cat

Sand cat (रेतिला बील्ली)

The sand cat (Felis margarita), also know as the sand dune cat, is the only cat living chiefly in true desert. This small cat is widely distributed in the deserts of North Africa. Starting in 2002, it was listen as near threatened on the IUCN Red List because the population was considered fragmented and small with a declining trend. It was downlisted to least concern in 2016. It's sandy to light grew fur, it is well camouflaged in a desert environment. The long hair covering the soles of it's feet insulates it's foot pads against the extremely hot and cold temperatures in deserts.

Baby of Sand cat (Kitten)

Kitten (बिलौटा)

Oestrus in female sand cats lasts from five to six days, during which they frequently call and scent mark. After a gestation of 59 to 66 days they give birth to a litter of tow to three kittens. They weigh 39 to 80g (1.4 to 2.8 oz) at birth, and have spotted pale yellow or reddish fur. By 4 weeks of age, the kitten can eliminate urine and faeces on their own, before this, they rely on the mum to stimulate them to excrete their waste. These cats have been reported to have 2 litters per year in parts of their territory in both March-April. They are sexually maturity around 10-12 months.

Scientific classification of Black-Footed cat

1. Kingdom. = Animalia

2. Phylum. = Chordata

3. Class. = Mammalia

4. Order. = Carnivora

5. Suborder. = Feliformia

6. Family. = Felidae

7. Sub family. = Felinae

8. Genus. = Felis

9. Species. = F. nigripes

10. Length. = 43 centimeters

11. Weight. = 1.9 kilograms

12. Speed. = 1.9 miles per hour

13. Black-Footed cat are found in = Botswana , Namibia , Africa , Savannas .

Black-Footed cat

Black-Footed cat (काले-पैर वाला बिल्ली)

The black-footed cat's vision is six times better than that of humans, aided by enormous eyes. It's also equipped with excellent night vision and impeccable hearing that can pick up even the tiniest sound. Despite its name, only the pads and underparts of the cat's feet are black. Coat colouration ranges from reddish-fawn (in the southern parts of Africa) to a much paler colour further north. The chin and throat are white, with distinct dark bands on the throat, and a black-tipped tail. This description helps a lot when differentiating it from an African wildcat. The black-footed cat is also solitary.

Baby of Black-Footed cat (Kitten)

Kitten (बिलौटा)

This tiny cat is perhaps the smallest of all wild cat species in Africa. The total length of its body is between 50-72 centimeters (including the tail). The male weighs between 1. 7-2.4 kilograms while the female is only 1-1. 6 kilograms. Kittens weigh a mere 60-90 g when born. Black-Footed cat mate in the fall, in August and September, giving birth to young in November to December in an underground den. Females may have multiple litters in a year and young have been recorded in dense as late as February.

Scientific classification of American Short-hair cat

1. Kingdom.	=	Animalia
2. Phylum.	=	Chordata
3. Class.	=	Mammalia
4. Order.	=	Carnivora
5. Suborder.	=	Feliformia
6. Family.	=	Felidae
7. Sub family.	=	Felinae
8. Genus.	=	Felis
9. Species.	=	F. catus
10. Length.	=	38.1 centimeters
11. Weight.	=	5.443 kilograms
12. Speed.	=	30 miles per hour

13. American Short-hair cat are found in = America .

American Short-hair cat

American Short-hair cat (अमरीकी छोटे बालो वाली बिल्ली)

The American Shorthair is a powerful cat. All components of this cat should be well developed. She has a broad chest, a muscular neck, strong jaws and a well-developed muzzle. Her legs are thick and strong. She looks like what she was originally meant to be, a cat to keep rodents out of the barn and the house. The coat of the American Shorthair is thick and dense. Her coat becomes much longer and thicker during the winter. The texture of her coat is relatively hard as it is meant as protection for her.

Baby of American short-Hair cat (Kitten)

Kitten (बिलौटा)

Puberty (the age at which animals can reproduce) in a female cat ranges from 4 to 12 months, with the average being 6 to 9 months. At puberty, cats are generally about 75% of their mature body weight. Domestic shorthair cats, as a breed, generally reach puberty earlier than domestic longhair cats. They generally have their kittens 58 to 65 days after they are bred. Generally, a cat has four to six kittens in each litter. The average cat could have three litters a year.

Scientific classification of British Short-hair cat

1. Kingdom. = Animalia
2. Phylum. = Chordata
3. Class. = Mammalia
4. Order. = Carnivora
5. Suborder. = Feliformia
6. Family. = Felidae
7. Sub family. = Felinae
8. Genus. = Felis
9. Species. = F.catus
10. Length. = 64 centimeter
11. Weight. = 7.7 kilogram
12. Speed. = 20 miles per hour
13. British Short-hair cat are found in = England.

British Short-hair cat

British Short-hair cat (ब्रिटिश छोटे बालों वाली बिल्ली)

The British Shorthair is a medium-sized to large cat and she is a very powerful one. She is heavily muscled and has heavy boning. She has a rounded, thick appearance. As a powerful cat, all components of this breed should be well developed. The British Shorthair has a broad chest, muscular neck, strong jaws and a well developed muzzle. The legs are thick and strong. The breed looks like what she originally was, a cat that was to keep rodents out of the barn and the house.

Baby of British Short-hair cat (Kitten)

Kitten (बिलौटा)

British shorthair cats are sexually mature in about eight months, after which they will be able to give birth. However, for the British shorthair's health, it is best to wait for it to grow up to one year old before mating and giving birth. At this time, the British shorthair's body functions Gradually mature, pregnancy and childbirth cause less harm to the body. If you give birth immediately after sexual maturity, stillbirth and dystocia are prone to occur.

Scientific classification of Bobtail cat

1. Kingdom. = Animalia

2. Phylum. = Chordata

3. Class. = Mammalia

4. Order. = Carnivora

5. Suborder. = Feliformia

6. Family. = Felidae

7. Sub family. = Felinae

8. Genus. = Felis

9. Species. = F.catus

10. Length. = 45. 72 centimeters

11. Weight. = 5. 897 kilograms

12. Speed. = 30 miles per hour

13. Bobtail cat are found in = America , Japan , Germany , Asia .

Bobtail cat

Bobtail cat (कट दुम वाली बिल्ली)

These cats are **playful, friendly, and intelligent**. They adore spending time with their family, and they typically get along great with kids, dogs, and other cats. Bobtails enjoy simple entertainment and fun, but they also appreciate a mental challenge. Bobtail is a breed of domestic cat. It is an uncommon breed of cat which developed in the late 1960s. Bobtails are known for their short bobbed tails, rugged appearance, and playful personalities. You can identify bobtail by its tail first and foremost. These cats have a stubby, bobbed tail that's only around one-third the length of a normal cat's tail.

Baby of Bobtail cat (Kitten)

Kitten (बिलौटा)

The American Bobtail, sometimes referred to as the Golden Retriever of the cat world, was first discovered in Arizona in the 1960s. This cat was bred with a non-pedigreed domestic cat, whose **kittens inherited their father's bobtail**. Bobtail cats are **a unique breed of domesticated cats** that get their unusual name thanks to their nub-like tail, which is the result of a genetic mutation and is about one-third the length of a normal cat's tail.

Scientific classification of Bengal cat

1. Kingdom.	=	Animalia
2. Phylum.	=	Chordata
3. Class.	=	Mammalia
4. Order.	=	Carnivora
5. Suborder.	=	Feliformia
6. Family.	=	Felidae
7. Sub family.	=	Felinae
8. Genus.	=	Felis
9. Species.	=	F. catus
10. Length.	=	40.64 centimeters
11. Weight.	=	6. 804 kilograms
12. Speed.	=	35 miles per hour

13. Bengal cat are found in = West Bengal .

Bengal cat

Bengal cat (बंगाल की बिल्ली)

The bengal is revered for its beautiful coat and outgoing personality , but these cats aren't for casual pet owners. The first Bengals were created by breeding Asian leopard cats with domestic cats. While documentation of the hybrid reaches back as early as the 1800s , the breed was perfected in the 1980s by Jean Sugden Mill. The treat of getting wet sends most cats clamoring for cover , but not the water-loving Bengal. These frisky felines will gladly drink right from the tap if allowed. Bengals are not typical , lazy house cats. They're very smart and need plenty of attention and toys to keep them occupied.

Baby of Bengal cat (Kitten)

Kitten (बिलौटा)

Females will come into heat every 2-3 weeks for 4-7 days at a time. This can vary. Some cats come into heat and do not come out until bred. Kittens are not born at convenient ... finding a veterinarian to help. Kittens born with problems. Some kittens are born in need of help immediately, some die. You need a good protocol for maintaining health. learning how to tube feed for those situations when needed, and feed kittens every two hours if mother cannot. Handle them daily, spending time around them, acclimate them to a normal human household and common occurrences.

Scientific classification of Sphynx Hairless cat

1. Kingdom. = Animalia
2. Phylum. = Chordata
3. Class. = Mammalia
4. Order. = Carnivora
5. Suborder. = Feliformia
6. Family. = Felidae
7. Sub family. = Felinae
8. Genus. = Felis
9. Species. = F. catus
10. Length. = 25 centimeters
11. Weight. = 5 kilograms
12. Speed. = 30 miles per hour
13. Sphynx Hairless cat are found in = Egypt , Canada , Ontario , Russia , Toronto .

Sphynx Hairless cat

Sphynx Hairless cat (स्फिंक्स बालों रहित बिल्ली)

The sphynx is a medium-sized cat with a striking appearance, identified by her hairless, wrinkled skin and large ears. She has a sleek, muscular body that is dence and heavy for her skin. The breed is medium sized but nicely muscled. Her head is triangular with wide-set eyes and prominent cheekbones that call back to the cats of ancient Egypt, a resemblance that inspired the naming of this breed. Apart for being hairless, the sphynx's most notable feature is her large, triangle-shaped ears that resemble those of a bat. The sphynx cat is an energetic, acrobatic performer who loves to show off for attention.

Baby of Sphynx Hairless cat (Kitten)

Kitten (बिलौटा)

At a time a female Sphynx cat gives birth to around **four kittens** in a litter. Hairlessness in cats is a **naturally occurring genetic mutation**, and the Sphynx was developed through selective breeding of these animals, starting in the 1960s. ... Because they have no fur, Sphynx cats lose body heat more readily than coated cats, making them both warm to the touch and prone to seeking out warm places.

Scientific classification of Siamese cat

1. Kingdom.	=	Animalia
2. Phylum.	=	Chordata
3. Class.	=	Mammalia
4. Order.	=	Carnivora
5. Suborder.	=	Feliformia
6. Family.	=	Felidae
7. Sub family.	=	Felinae
8. Genus.	=	Felis
9. Species.	=	F. catus
10. Length.	=	36 centimeters
11. Weight.	=	5 kilograms
12. Speed.	=	30 miles per hour

13. Siamese cat are found in = Thailand, England, America.

Siamese cat

Siamese cat (स्यामी बिल्ली)

Siamese cats are one of the oldest domesticated cats in the world! The breed originated in Thailand (formerly known as Siam) in the 14th century, but it didn't make its debut in the states until the 19th century. The breed originated in Thailand (formerly known as Siam) in the 14th century, but it didn't make its debut in the states until the 19th century. Famous for their ballerina-esque bodies, Siamese cats are sleek and lithe. They have piercing baby blue eyes, large ears, and a coat that comes in four different shades—seal, chocolate, blue, and lilac.

Baby of Siamese cat (Kitten)

Kitten (बिलौटा)

Siamese cats typically only have **four to six babies**. Siamese cats, however, have a slightly longer pregnancy, usually lasting **around 67 days**. **Siamese kitties are thin by nature**, so it can be hard to tell when their breed qualities stop and health concerns start. As a general rule, a male Siamese should weigh around 9.9lbs – 12.1lbs and a female 7.7lbs – 10.6lbs. If they fall even 10% under this threshold, then their weight is a cause for concern.

Scientific classification of Scottish fold cat

1. Kingdom.	=	Animalia
2. Phylum.	=	Chordata
3. Class.	=	Mammalia
4. Order.	=	Carnivora
5. Suborder.	=	Feliformia
6. Family.	=	Felidae
7. Sub family.	=	Felinae
8. Genus.	=	Felis
9. Species.	=	F. catus
10 Length.	=	25.4 centimeters
11. Weight.	=	5.443 kilograms
12. Speed.	=	30 miles per hour

13. Scottish fold cat are found in = Perthshire, Scotland .

Scottish fold cat

Scottish fold cat (स्कॉटिश फोल्ड बिल्ली)

Scottish fold cats are known for their trademark folded ears that make for an adorable look. They have round faces and big round eyes, and their folded ears make them appear even rounder. In fact, they're often compared to teddy bears or owls. Because of their cute appearance and sweet temperament, they're very sought-after and beloved by many. Their ears are their signature feature, and they're completely fascinating.

Baby of Scottish fold cat (Kitten)

Kitten (बिलौटा)

While Scottish fold cats are known for their signature folded ears, they're actually born with straight ears. The fold begins to develop when the kitten is between 18 and 24 days old, but only if they have the gene that is responsible for the fold. Oftentimes, their ears will stay straight, in which case they're known as Scottish shorthairs. In general, about 50% of a litter with one Scottish fold parent will have folded ears and the other 50% will not.

Scientific classification of American Long-hair cat

1. Kingdom. = Animalia

2. Phylum. = Chordata

3. Class. = Mammalia

4. Order. = Carnivora

5. Suborder. = Feliformia

6. Family. = Felidae

7. Sub family. = Felinae

8. Genus. = Felis

9. Species. = F. catus

10. Length. = 45.72 centimeters

11. Weight. = 6.804 kilograms

12. Speed. = 30 miles per hour

13. American Long-hair cat are found in = America.

American Long-hair cat

American Long-hair cat (अमेरिकी लंबी-बालो वाली बिल्ली)

American Longhair cats likely first came to America from England with the first settlers. The colonists had them on their ships to protect the grain from mice and other threats. The American longhair is not a specific cat breed, although aficionados are encouraging cat fancy associations to recognize this unique feline. For now, the term American longhair is used to indicate a cross between a Persian cat and an American shorthair cat.

Baby of American Long-hair cat (Kitten)

Kitten (बिलौटा

The breeding season in cats lasts **almost year-round**. Heat cycles can start as early as four or five months in a female kitten. Heat cycles in cats repeat every two to three weeks until the cat is spayed or becomes pregnant. cat's pregnancy lasts about 63-65 days. So, a cat can have kittens when they are only 6 months old.

Scientific classification of Burmese cat

1. Kingdom. = Animalia

2. Phylum. = Chordala

3. Class. = Mammalia

4. Order. = Carnivora

5. Suborder. = Feliformia

6. Family. = Felidae

7. Sub family. = Felinae

8. Genus. = Felis

9. Species. = F. calus

10. Length. = 46 centimeters

11. Weight. = 6 kilograms

12. Speed. = 30 miles per hour

13. Burmese cat are found in = America , Myanmar , Burma , France , India .

Burmese cat

Burmese cat (बर्मी बिल्ली)

The Burmese cat is a breed of domestic cat, originating in Burma, believed to have its roots near the Thai-Burma border and developed in the United States and Britain. Most modern Burmese are descendants of one female cat called Wong Mau, which was brought from Burma to America in 1930 and bred with American Siamese. The Burmese cat is medium sized, with a rounded head and an elegant yet well-muscled body. The breed is not as large and sturdy as the British Shorthair cat breed nor as slender and dainty as Siamese cats.

Baby of Burmese cat (Kitten)

Kitten (बिलौटा)

About three weeks after mating you should expect your queen to "pink-up" if she is pregnant. This is characterised by a reddening of the nipples and the surrounding hair receding,particularly noticeable in maiden queens. For the next six weeks she may sleep and eat more than usual. Puberty occurs around the age of 9 months in the Burmese cat. An average litter may contain 6 kittens, meaning its prolificacy is slightly higher than the average of other cat breeds.

Scientific classification of Maine coon cat

1. Kingdom.	=	Animalia
2. Phylum.	=	Chordata
3. Class.	=	Mammalia
4. Order.	=	Carnivora
5. Suborder.	=	Feliformia
6. Family.	=	Felidae
7. Sub family.	=	Felinae
8. Genus.	=	Felis
9. Species.	=	F. catus
10. Length.	=	100 centimeters
11. Weight.	=	8. 2 kilograms
12. Speed.	=	25 miles per hour

13. Manie coon cat are found in = America , Europe , England .

Maine coon cat

Maine coon cat (मेन कून बिल्ली)

Maine Coon cats are as distinctive as their names. If you ever see one, you'll surely recognize it again next time you come across it. There's a quality about these animals that exude warmth and coziness, and if you ask any cat owner who lives with a Maine Coon, they'll tell you exactly how cuddly and comfortable these cats could be. The name Maine Coon has many folk tales associated with it. One story states that an English seafarer named Captain Charles Coon kept longhaired cats aboard his ship. Every time his ship docked, his cats supposedly mated with other feral cats in the local area.

Baby of Maine coon cat (Kitten)

Kitten (बिलौटा)

The Maine Coon mating age is usually **around five or six months old**. This is when a cat reaches sexual maturity and is ready to start finding a mate. A female Maine Coon that becomes pregnant before she is fully grown can experience stunted growth and might even be more at risk for a dangerous pregnancy and birth. The average Maine Coon litter size is about four or five kittens, and they rarely have litters of more than six.

Scientific classification of Turkish Angora cat

1. Kingdom.	=	Animalia
2. Phylum.	=	Chordata
3. Class.	=	Mammalia
4. Order.	=	Carnivora
5. Suborder.	=	Feliformia
6. Family.	=	Felidae
7. Sub family.	=	Felinae
8. Genus.	=	Felis
9. Species.	=	Felis Catus
10. Length.	=	41 centimetres
11. Weight.	=	4.5 kilogram
12. Speed.	=	30 miles per hour

13. Japanese bobtail cat are found in = Turkey.

Turkish Angora cat

Turkish Angora cat (तुर्की अंगोरा बिल्ली)

Turkish Angora is small to medium-sized cat that originates from Turkey. It was created in 15th century and introduced to Europe one century later via trade routes (one of the first longhair cats that arrived to Europe). According to one theory, Turkish Angora was brought to Europe by Vikings. Turkish Angora was nearly wiped out from Europe at the beginning of the 20th century due to frequent interbreeding with Persian cat, as a result of high demand for cats with long fur (that were very popular back then).

Baby of Turkish Angora cat (Kitten)

Kitten (बिलौटा)

Young Turkish Angora's reach sexual maturity around 8 to 12 months. Pregnancy usually lasts 56 to 71 days with litters of between 3 and 5 kittens. The Angora is a natural breed, not manmade, and existed in Turkey at least as far back as the 15th century.

Scientific classification of Manx cat

1. Kingdom. = Animalia

2. Phylum. = Chordata

3. Class. = Mammalia

4. Order. = Carnivora

5. Suborder. = Feliformia

6. Family. = Felidae

7. Sub family. = Felinae

8. Genus. = Felis

9. Species. = Felis Catus

10. Length. = 41 centimetres

11. Weight. = 5.4 kilogram

12. Japanese bobtail cat are found in = Isle of Man.

Manx cat

Manx cat (मान द्वीप का बिल्ली)

Manx cats carry one gene for a full tail, and one for taillessness. This means that two Manx cats can mate and produce a kitten that's a typical long-tailed feline. Sadly, kittens that inherit the taillessness gene from both parents will likely die before birth. That's why some people have nicknamed the Manx gene "the lethal gene." Typically, a Manx cat's eyes are gold, copper, green, hazel, blue, or odd-eyed. The Manx is a rounded cat with a round head, round eyes, a roundness at the whisker pads, and a round rump. The ears form a rocker shape when viewed from behind.

Baby of Manx cat (Kitten)

Kitten (बिलौटा)

The mating of two Manx cats yields two Manx kittens for each normal, long-tailed kitten, rather than three-to-one as would be predicted from Mendelian genetics. If your cat was recently in heat and had access to an intact (unneutered) male cat, there's a chance that she is pregnant. A pregnant queen will display both physical and personality changes that will become more evident around three weeks after breeding. The gestation period for cats runs **64 to 66 days**.

Scientific classification of Munchkin cat

1. Kingdom.	=	Animalia
2. Phylum.	=	Chordata
3. Class.	=	Mammalia
4. Order.	=	Carnivora
5. Suborder.	=	Feliformia
6. Family.	=	Felidae
7. Sub family.	=	Felinae
8. Genus.	=	Felis
9. Species.	=	Felis Catus
10. Length.	=	45.72 centimetres
11. Weight.	=	4.5 kilogram

12. Japanese bobtail cat are found in = America , India.

Munchkin cat

Munchkin cat (मुंचकिन बिल्ली)

Like many unusual cat types (the Cornish Rex and the Manx, to name a few), the Munchkin breed arose from a spontaneous genetic mutation. The Munchkin's short legs are caused by an autosomal dominant gene, which causes the long bones in a cat's legs to grow shorter. A cat only needs one copy of the gene to inherit short legs and to pass the trait along to its kittens. Throughout the 20th century, various individuals documented sightings of short-legged feral cats in Great Britain, Russia, and New England.

Baby of Munchkin cat (Kitten)

Kitten (बिलौटा)

Munchkin cats originated when a lady found that one cat often would give ve birth to cats with the munchkin traits. She carefully worked the breeding of these traits into a specific line and it too something like 20 or more for it to receive recognition and formal classification through the CFAA. If a Munchkin kitten get pregnant for a regular cat, there are high chances the kitten will be Munchkin kittens as the gene that make the bones shorter are present in the mother.

Scientific classification of Cornish Rex cat

1. Kingdom.	=	Animalia
2. Phylum.	=	Chordata
3. Class.	=	Mammalia
4. Order.	=	Carnivora
5. Suborder.	=	Feliformia
6. Family.	=	Felidae
7. Sub family.	=	Felinae
8. Genus.	=	Felis
9. Species.	=	Felis Catus
10. Length.	=	43 centimetres
11. Weight.	=	4.5 kilogram

12. Japanese bobtail cat are found in = United Kingdom.

Cornish Rex cat

Cornish Rex cat (कोर्निश रेक्स बिल्ली)

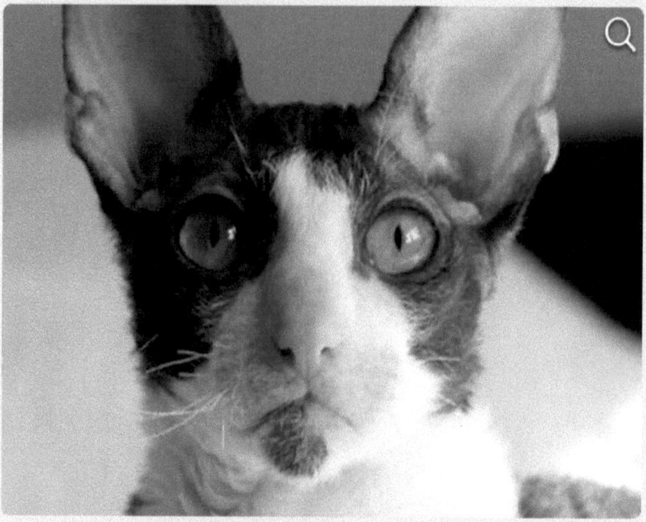

In 1950, a woman named Nina Ennismore who lived in Cornwall, England, discovered that her domestic British shorthair had given birth to a quirky-looking male kitten with tightly curled fur. As the cat grew older, he also developed big, bat-like ears, and a lithe frame reminiscent of an English Greyhound. Over the years, breeders have outcrossed the Cornish Rex breed with other types of cats, including Siamese, Burmese, Russian Blue, and British Shorthairs, to improve the Rex's health and stamina.

Baby of Cornish Rex cat (Kitten)

Kitten (बिलौटा)

A Cornish Rex cat breed has an average litter size of four to six and curly-coated kittens are born after a gestation period of 71 days. The first Cornish Rex kitten was born through natural mutation in 1950 on a farm in Cornwall, England. A Cornish Rex's reproduction is not different from any other cat's. These pet cat breeds have multiple estrous cycles throughout the year and the mating season generally depends on the temperature and location.

Scientific classification of California Spangled cat

1. Kingdom. = Animalia

2. Phylum. = Chordata

3. Class. = Mammalia

4. Order. = Carnivora

5. Suborder. = Feliformia

6. Family. = Felidae

7. Sub family. = Felinae

8. Genus. = Felis

9. Species. = F. catus

10. Length. = 25.4 centimeter

11. Weight. = 6.804 kilogram

12. Speed. = 30 miles per hour

13. California Spangled cat are found in = California.

California Spangled cat

California Spangled cat (कैलिफ़ोर्निया स्पैंगल्ड बिल्ली)

The **California Spangled** is a breed of domestic cat that was bred to resemble spotted wild cats, like the ocelot and leopard. They were originally bred in the 1980s and were only ever a rare breed, with only 58 ever being registered. The California Spangled cat was one of the first domestic cats bred to resemble exotic wild spotted cat species. And they were launched into the public imagination like no other breed before them. They are full of energy.

Baby of California Spangled cat (Kitten)

Kitten (बिलौटा)

Although they were initially expensive due to their rarity, the breed has since been overshadowed by the Ocicat and Bengal. The first California Spangled cats were created by crossing several breeds including Abyssinian, Siamese, American shorthair, British shorthair, and Angora cats. The breed was finally perfected in 1985, and the cats were introduced to the public in 1986 when they graced the cover of the Neiman Marcus Christmas catalog.

Scientific classification of Cymric cat

1. Kingdom.	=	Animalia
2. Phylum.	=	Chordata
3. Class.	=	Mammalia
4. Order.	=	Carnivora
5. Sub order.	=	Feliformia
6. Family.	=	Felidae
7. Sub family.	=	Felinae
8. Genus.	=	Felis
9. Species.	=	F.catus
10.Length.	=	45.72 centimeter
11.Weight.	=	5.897 kilogram
12.Speed.	=	22 miles per hour

13.Cymric cat are found in = Canada.

Cymric cat

Cymric cat (सिमरिक बल्ली)

The Cymric is a medium-sized cat that is stocky and heavily boned. The Cymric can appear larger than she is or you may not realize how heavy she can actually be when she is fully mature. *The Cymric is a rounded cat with a round head, round eyes, a roundness at the whisker pads, and a round rump. The way the ears are placed forms a rocker shape when viewed from behind. The hind end of her is higher than the. front, which is apparent when she is standing. Not every Cymric is completely tailless. On a completely tailless Cymric, no protuberance can be felt. These cats are called rumpies.*

Baby of Cymric cat (Kitten)

Kitten (बिलौटा)

Cymric cat breed is solidly built and chunky with a similar body type to the British Shorthair cat breed with large eyes and widely spaced ears. The lack of a tail is the breed's most outstanding feature. Its hind legs are longer than the front legs. The Cymric cat's hair is thick and provides a layer of padding over the main body, adding to the round appearance. A rabbit-like hop can sometimes be seen in Cymric cats because of the spinal deformity, similar to spinabifida, which associated with the taillessness.

Scientific classification of Devon Rex cat

1. Kingdom. = Animalia

2. Phylum. = Chordata

3. Class. = Mammalia

4. Order. = Carnivora

5. Suborder. = Feliformia

6. Family. = Felidae

7. Sub family. = Felinae

8. Genus. = Felis

9. Species. = F. catus

10. Length. = 46 centimeters

11. Weight. = 4 kilograms

12. Speed. = 30 miles per hour

13. Devon Rex cat are found in = England.

Devon Rex cat

Devon Rex cat (शैतानी रेक्स बिल्ली)

A Devon Rex cat generally loves people and can easily become attach to your family and friends. A kitten born in Devon, England in 1959 named Kirlee was first thought to have the same genes as the Cornish Rex. However, test breeding found out that Kirlee was certainly unique and a result of a very natural genetic mutation. Though this seems odd, but a Devon Rex loves to stay level on the head of the person it likes. Due to this strange liking, the Devon Rex is usually seen situated on the shoulder of its favorite person considering that shoulders are in level with the head.

Baby of Devon Rex cat (Kitten)

Kitten (बिलौटा)

It's widely accepted that this breed of cat has its origins in the Devonshire region of England in 1960. A **female domestic short-haired cat mated with a stray tom cat with a peculiar curl to his coat**. The resulting litter produced one curly-coated kitten that was immediately noticed for his unique fur and named Kirlee.

Scientific classification of Bombay cat

1. Kingdom. = Animalia

2. Phylum. = Chordata

3. Class. = Mammalia

4. Order. = Carnivora

5. Suborder. = Feliformia

6. Family. = Felidae

7. Sub family. = Felinae

8. Genus. = Felis

9. Species. = F.catus

10. Length. = 56 centimetre

11. Weight. = 6.804 kilogram

12. Speed. = 29.826 miles per hour

13. Bombay cat are found in = Bombay.

Bombay cat

Bombay cat (बंबई की बिल्ली)

The Bombay cat is not a breed that occurs naturally. They are a man made kind that was bred from combining a few different varieties to come up with the perfect genetic combination that gives them their lovely appearance. They do feature an exotic look and they tend to have mysterious personalities. When you look into their eyes it's almost a supernatural experience , so of course , they had to be named after a place that would offer a description of this amazing cat. They are named after Bombay , the exotic port in the country of India.

Baby of Bombay cat (Kitten)

Kitten (बिलौटा)

Bombay **females have litters of 3 kittens on average.** The only cross breeding permitted are those between the Bombay and the sepia black American Burmese. The **Bombay cat** is a type of short-haired cat developed by breeding sable Burmese and black American Shorthair cats, to produce a cat of mostly Burmese type, but with a sleek, panther-like black coat. Bombay is the name given to black cats of the Asian group.

Scientific classification of Tabby cat

1. Kingdom. = Animalia

2. Phylum. = Chordata

3. Class. = Mammalia

4. Order. = Carnivora

5. Suborder. = Feliformia

6. Family. = Felidae

7. Sub family. = Felinae

8. Genus. = Felis

9. Species. = F.catus

10. Length. = 40.64 centimetre

11. Weight. = 4.536 kilogram

12. Speed. = 30 miles per hour

13. Tabby cat are found in = Egypt.

Tabby cat

Tabby cat (धारीदार बिल्ली)

Tabby cats got their name by being compared to silk from the "Attabiy" district in Baghdad, and the 14th century Middle French term for it was "atabis," which then became "tabis," and Tabbies are not an actual breed, but rather, the name is a way to describe the unique markings on their coats that set them apart. So "tabby cat" refers to a category of cats, not a recognized breed. eventually our English word, "tabby." Tabby patterns assist in camouflage when cats are hiding in tall grass or brush hunting for prey.

Baby of Tabby cat (Kitten)

Kitten (बिलौटा)

When a female kitten approaches maturity, her reproductive system kicks into gear. In general, cats become sexually mature as they approach 80% of their adult body weight. Most often this happens between five and seven months of age. The feline reproductive system is designed to produce kittens during the warmer months. This means that as the days start to grow longer, more and more cats start to cycle.

Scientific classification of Birman cat

1. Kingdom.	=	Animalia
2. Phylum.	=	Chordata
3. Class.	=	Mammalia
4. Order.	=	Carnivora
5. Suborder.	=	Feliformia
6. Family.	=	Felidae
7. Sub family.	=	Felinae
8. Genus.	=	Felis
9. Species.	=	F.catus
10. Length.	=	45.72 centimeter
11. Weight.	=	6.804 kilogram
12. Speed.	=	30 miles per hour

13. Birman cat are found in = Europe, Australia, America, New Zealand.

Birman cat

Birman cat (बिरमान बिल्ली)

Birman , also know as sacred cat of Burma , is a type of semi-longhair domestic cat that originates from Burma. It was probably created by mixing Siamese with Angora or Persian cats. Birman has been introduced to Europe in 1919 and to the USA in 1959. Birman has broad , rounded head with prominent sapphire-blue eyes , medium-sized ears and stocky , powerful , rectangular body. Name "Birmin" originates from a French word for Burma - Birmanie.

Baby of Birman cat (Kitten)

Kitten (बिलौटा)

Birman cats reach sexual maturity around the time they are four to five months old. Their gestation period lasts for **about 64 to 66 days.** Female cats show certain traits like nesting, sleeping more, and an increase in appetite that indicates that they are carrying kittens.

Scientific classification of Toyger cat

1. Kingdom. = Animalia

2. Phylum. = Chordata

3. Class. = Mammalia

4. Order. = Carnivora

5. Suborder. = Feliformia

6. Family. = Felidae

7. Sub family. = Felinae

8. Genus. = Felis

9. Species. = F.catus

10. Length. = 61 centimetre

11. Weight. = 6.804 kilogram

12. Speed. = 29.826 miles per hour

13. Toyger cat are found in = America.

Toyger cat

Toyger cat (टोयगर बिल्ली)

Toyger isn't a name that beats around the bush. Without even seeing one, you know right away this cat is supposed to look like a tiny tiger. A toy tiger, if you will. Created in the 1980s, the toyger is a cat bread specifically to replicate not only the striped markings of its jungle cat namesake, but other physical traita as well. This has resulted in a muscular, athletic cat with a rolling gait that looks like she'd be more at home in an Indian jungle than a living room. There aren't actually any tiger genes in their DNA.

Baby of Toyger cat (Kitten)

Kitten (बिलौटा)

These kitties were also bred to be friendly and social , and they love to be around their humans and other furry friends. However, like other felines, the Toyger female also has her estrus (heat) cycle. Mating during the cycle will make the female Toyger cat pregnant. The gestation period lasts **between 58-67 days**, and they usually have a litter size of four to six Toyger kittens.

Scientific classification of Savannah cat

1. Kingdom. = Animalia

2. Phylum. = Chordata

3. Class. = Mammalia

4. Order. = Carnivora

5. Suborder. = Feliformia

6. Family. = Felidae

7. Sub family. = Felinae

8. Genus. = Felis

9. Species. = Felis Catus

10. Length. = 56 centimetres

11. Weight. = 8 kilogram

12. Speed. = 50 miles per hour

13. Japanese bobtail cat are found in = Africa.

Savannah cat

Savannah cat (सवाना की बिल्ली)

Savannah cats are the result of crossing a domestic cat and a Serval- a medium-sized, large-eared wild African cat. These first crosses are then bred again and the resulting cats are termed domestic and usually have a short spotted coat. The Manx is a rounded cat with a round head, round eyes, a roundness at the whisker pads, and a round rump. The ears form a rocker shape when viewed from behind. The hind end of the Manx is higher than the front, which is apparent when she is standing.

Baby of Savannah cat (Kitten)

Kitten (बिलौटा)

The normal development (gestation) is between 58 to 65 days or about 9 weeks. The usual number of kittens that are born can be between 1 to as many as 8 in the litter. The norm (average) number of kittens is 3 to 5. A Savannah kitten is a hybrid of a domestic cat and the serval. This new breed grew in popularity among breeders in the later 1990s, and in 2001 it was accepted as a new registered breed by the International Cat Association. It wasn't until May of 2012, that TICA made it a championship breed.

Scientific classification of Russian Blue cat

1. Kingdom. = Animalia
2. Phylum. = Chordata
3. Class. = Mammalia
4. Order. = Carnivora
5. Suborder. = Feliformia
6. Family. = Felidae
7. Sub family. = Felinae
8. Genus. = Felis
9. Species. = Felis Catus
10. Length. = 25.4 centimetres
11. Weight. = 6.804 kilograms
12. Speed. = 30 miles per hour
13. Russian Blue cat are found in = Russia.

Russian Blue cat

Russian Blue cat (रसिया की नीली बिल्ली)

Whith their shimmery blue coats , striking emerald eyes , and possible ties to Russian czars , Russian Blue cats can't help but have a certain air of elegance. Russian Blue cats belong to the same classification as the British Blue cat , the Chartreux of France , and the Korat of Thailand. However , they are a distinct breed with unique characteristics. Russian Blues stand out because of their bright green eyes. They are also slenderer in build with a wedge-shaped head , while their blue cousins tend to be stockier and rounder in the face. Russian Blue cats grow to be approximately 10 inches tall.

Baby of Russian Blue cat (Kitten)

Kitten (बिलौटा)

However, if you've spent time with one of these gorgeous kittens, you know that they're as sensetive and caring as they come — and clever, too! In fact, the more you lern about Russian Blues, the more there is to love.

Russian Blue cats grow to be approximately 10 inches tall and weigh 7-15 pounds. If well cared for, they can live 15-20 years — If not longer! These kittens are also referred to as Archangel Blues, Foreign Blues, or Maltese Cats.

Scientific classification of Japanese bobtail cat

1. Kingdom. = Animalia

2. Phylum. = Chordata

3. Class. = Mammalia

4. Order. = Carnivora

5. Suborder. = Feliformia

6. Family. = Felidae

7. Sub family. = Felinae

8. Genus. = Felis

9. Species. = Felis Catus

10. Length. = 22.86 centimetres

11. Weight. = 4.5 kilogram

12. Speed. = 30 miles per hour

13. Japanese bobtail cat are found in = Japan.

Japanese Bobtail cat

Japanese Bobtail cat (जापानी कट दुम वाली बिल्ली)

Cat fanciers believe that the Japanese Bobtail is an ancient breed. According to popular belief, Buddhist monks originally owned the kitties. In the 1600s, rodents infested silkworm barns and threatened the country's lucrative silk trade. Authorities ordered people to set their cats loose on the streets to take out the vermin. Over time, the Japanese Bobtail became the country's de facto street cat. Japanese Bobtails are considered to be good luck.

Baby of Japanese Bobtail cat (Kitten)

Kitten (बिलौटा)

Japanese Bobtails are very strong and healthy cats. They usually have litters of three to four kittens that are large for newborns. Compared to other breeds, the kittens are active earlier, walk earlier, and start getting into trouble earlier! This breed has a low kitten mortality rate and a high disease resistance rate. Kittens are never born tailless, nor are they born with full tails.

Scientific classification of Somali cat

1. Kingom.	=	Animalia
2. Phylum.	=	Chordata
3. Class.	=	Mammalia
4. Order.	=	Carnivora
5. Suborder.	=	Feliformia
6. Family.	=	Felidae
7. Sub family.	=	Felinae
8. Genus.	=	Felis
9. Species.	=	Felis Catus
10. Length.	=	27.94 centimeter
11. Weight.	=	5 kilogram
12. Speed.	=	30 miles per hour

13. Somali cat are found in = Britan, Africa, Arabia.

Somali cat

Somali cat (सोमाली बिल्ली)

The Somali has been given the nickname "fox cat" because of his bushy tail. The Somali's coat can come in chocolate, blue, cinnamon, ruddy, lilac, fawn, or any silver variation of those colors. The Somali has large almond-shaped eyes that can come in an intense green or rich copper. The Somali is a very well proportioned, medium-sized, muscular cat. Somali, like Abyssinians, could develop a hereditary health issue called pyruvate kinase deficiency causing intermittent anemia.

Baby of Somali cat (Kitten)

Kitten (बिलौटा)

Some of the kittens born in the Abyssinian litters seemed to be long haired. Since long hair was not a trait desirable in Abyssinian, the long haired kittens born were altered and placed as pets. However, many breeders loved the way the long hair looked on Abyssinian cats and, in the late 1960s, these breeders created a longhaired version of the Abyssinian and called her the Somali. The beautiful ticked coat can be seen on the Somali just as it can on the Abyssinian.

Scientific classification of Raga muffin cat

1 . Kingdom = Animalia

2. Phylum. = Chordata

3. Class. = Mammalia

4. Order. = Carnivora

5. Suborder. = Feliformia

6. Family. = Felidae

7. Sub family. = Felinae

8. Genus. = Felis

9. Species. = F. catus

10. Length. = 46 centimeters

11. Weight. = 9. 072 kilograms

12. Speed. = 29. 95 miles per hour

13. Raga muffin cat are found in = California.

Raga Muffin cat

Raga Muffin cat (रागामफिन बिल्ली)

Raga Muffin has a medium-sized head but her fur makes her face appear large. The ears are also medium sized and are set on the sides of the head to continue the triangular look of the face. The legs are long and strong. The chin should be well developed and the oval eyes should be blue. Raga Muffin comes in various colours and patterns. Some of these colour patterns are the same as those of the ragdoll. The coat on the Raga Muffin can vary in length from semi-long to long.

It is soft , plush and silky. They are 33rd popular feline.

Baby of Raga Muffin cat (Kitten)

Kitten (बिलौटा)

Raga Muffin kittens are actually born white and develop a colour pattern as they mature. These gentle giants are one of the largest cat breeds. Raga Muffins are the 33rd most popular feline.

The breed can be prone to a condition know as heterochromia , meaning they have two different colored eyes. They can live to the ripe old age of 18. It can take four years for these full sized felines to reach complete physical maturity.

Scientific classification of Himalayan cat

1. Kingdom. = Animalia

2. Phylum. = Chordata

3. Class. = Mammalia

4. Order. = Carnivora

5. Suborder. = Feliformia

6. Family. = Felidae

7. Sub family. = Felinae

8. Genus. = Felis

9. Species. = F. catus

10. Length. = 48 centimeters

11. Weight. = 5 kilograms

12. Speed. = 30 miles per hour

13. Himalayan cat are found in = Himalayas.

Himalayan cat

Himalayan cat (हिमालयी बिल्ली)

Himalayan cats have been jokingly labeled Persian in a Saimese costume. While that's an adorable image, of course in its true. Weather or not Himalayas are a distinct breed - there is some debate - these sweet, docile longhair have enough lovable characteristics to celebrate them for the uniquely special kittens they are. Himalayas are a medium-sized sub-breed of longhair cat. They are almost identical to Persians except that they have brilliant blue eyes and the colorpoint markings of a Siamese. That means they have creamy bodies with a darker face, ears, feet and tail.

Baby of Himalayan cat (Kitten)

Kitten (बिलौटा)

A Himalayan's pregnancy should last about 63 days. Your vet can either palpate (feel) for pregnancy at about 21 days, or do an ultrasound test to confirm pregnancy and estimate how many kittens. Three to four kittens are a usual litter size for a Himalayan. Prepare a safe, quiet place for queening (giving birth). These sweet, docile longhair have enough lovable characteristics to celebrate them for the uniquely special kittens they are. These kittens can be shy, and they prefer a calm environment.

Scientific classification of Bay cat

1. Kingdom. = Animalia

2. Phylum. = Chordata

3. Class. = Mammalia

4. Order. = Carnivora

5. Suborder. = Feliformia

6. Family. = Felidae

7. Sub family. = Felinae

8. Genus. = Catopuma

9. Species. = C. badia

10. Length. = 67 centimetre

11. Weight. = 4 kilogram

12. Bay cat are found in = Borneo.

Bay cat

Bay cat (खाड़ी की बिल्ली)

Bay cat is one of the most mysterious and rarest species of wild cats in the world. This species lives only on the island of Borneo. It can be found in forests, mangroves, swamps and areas near the rivers. Bay cat can survive on the altitude of 5 900 feet. All scientific evidences about bay cats were based on the skulls and skins collected from the wild and on the less than 25 cats recorded by camera. Major threat for the survival of bay cats is habitat loss due to intense deforestation. Researchers estimate that there are roughly 2500 bay cats remaining in the wild. Bay cats are listed as endangered species.

Baby of Bay cat (Kitten)

Kitten (बिलौटा)

There is no information on reproduction including from captivity; there are no captive Bay Cats at the time of writing and the species has never bred in captivity. As they are difficult to observe in the wild.

Scientific classification of Marbled cat

1. Kingdom. = Animalia

2. Phylum. = Chordata

3. Class. = Mammalia

4. Order. = Carnivora

5. Suborder. = Feliformia

6. Family. = Felidae

7. Sub family. = Felinae

8. Genus. = Pardofelis

9. Species. = P. marmorata

10. Length. = 52 centimeters

11. Weight. = 3.2 kilogram

12. Speed. = 36 miles per hour

13. Marbled cat are found in = Himalayas , Indomalaya , China , Sumatra , Borneo.

Marbled cat

Marbled cat (मार्बल वाली बिल्ली)

The Marbled Cat is like a miniature version of the Clouded Leopard, weighing between 9-18 pounds and reaching lengths of 32-46 inches. It has thick, soft fur, which varies from brownish gray through yellow to reddish brown in color, and is covered in large blotches, which are paler in the center. There are black spots on its limbs and some black lines on the head and neck. The Marbled Cat has a short, more rounded head than other felines, with a wide forehead and large pupils. Like the Clouded Leopard, the Marbled Cat also has relatively enlarged upper canines.

Baby of Marbled cat (Kitten)

Kitten (बिलौटा)

On a few occasions marbled cats have given birth in captivity, with 2 litters yielding 2 kittens each and another litter of 4 kittens. Estrus occurs monthly, without seasonal variation in captive animals. Once pregnant , gestation lasts from 66 to 82 days in marbled cats. Captive kittens can eat solid food by 59 days of age in captivity, which may indicate the earliest onset of weaning in the wild. In addition to gestation, lactation, and food supplementation, there is likely time involved in teaching kittens to hunt leaving only enough time for a single litter per year.

Scientific classification of Puma

1. Kingdom. = Animalia

2. Phylum. = Chordata

3. Class. = Mammalia

4. Order. = Carnivora

5. Suborder. = Feliformia

6. Family. = Felidae

7. Sub family. = Felinae

8. Genus. = Puma

9. Species. = Felis concolor

10 Length. = 240. 792 centimeters

11.Weight. = 100 kilograms

12.Speed. = 50 miles per hour

13 Puma are found in = America , Mexico , Florida , Canada .

Puma

Puma (प्यूमा)

The Puma is the world's fourth largest cat, and is even biggest than some of the true big cats. The Puma holds the Guinness World Record for animal with the most number of names. Pumas can begin to reproduce from 2 to 3 years old. The life expectancy of the puma is approximately 10 years. Unlike other big cats, the puma has a slime body, similar to a house cat, but on a much large scale. In fact, in colloquial terms, the Patagonians refer to pumas as gatos. The puma's camouflauge allows it to blend in with the rocks and shrubs on the Patagonian pampa.

Baby of Puma (Cubs)

Cubs (शावक)

Pumas can begin to reproduce from 2 to 3 years old, and normally hace 2 or 3 cubs at a time. At six months old, cubs hunt for small prey of the own. They learn quickly. Cubs will leave their mother to establish their own territory at around tow years old. One litter of cubs is born every tow to three years. Pumas learn to climb the tree early in their life. When cubs are born, they have sports, blue eyes, and rings around their tails. The sports go away as they grow older. Cubs are kept within their maternal dens, caves or alcoves, a place closely surrounded with buses, rocks, and trees.

Scientific classification of Rusty-spotted cat

1. Kingdom. = Animalia
2. Phylum. = Chordata
3. Class. = Mammalia
4. Order. = Carnivora
5. Suborder. = Feliformia
6. Family. = Felidae
7. Subfamily. = Felinae
8. Genus. = Prionailurus
9. Species. = P. rubiginosus
10. Length. = 41 centimeters
11. Weight. = 1.4 kilogram
12. Speed. = 50 miles per hour
13. Rusty-spotted cat are found in = India , Nepal , Sri Lanka.

Rusty-spotted cat

Rusty-spotted cat (मोरचे के रंग का धब्बेदार बिल्ली)

This rare cat has short, brownish gray fur tinged with a rufous color. The face is marked with two dark streaks on each cheek and four dark stripes extending from above the eyes backward between the ears and to the shoulders. The back and flanks are marked with elongated blotches of rust-brown and spots that pattern the fur. The cat's belly, chest, and throat are white and marked with large dark spots and bars. The ears are small and rounded. The rusty-spotted cat is distributed in southern India and Sri Lanka.

Baby of Rusty-spotted cat (Kitten)

Kitten (बिलौटा)

At birth, the kittens weigh just 60 to 77 g (2.1 to 2.7 oz), and are marked with rows of black spots. They reach sexual maturity at around 68 weeks, by which time they have developed the distinctive adult coat pattern of rusty blotches. Rusty-spotted cats will mate **year-round**. The gestation period is about 67 days, and one or two kittens are born in a secluded den, like a shallow cave. Young begin to venture forth from the den at around 28 to 32 days. A litter of one to three kittens is born in a secluded den after a gestation of **approximately 67 days**.

Scientific classification of Geoffroy's cat

1. Kingdom. = Animalia

2. Phylum. = Chordata

3. Class. = Mammalia

4. Order. = Carnivora

5. Suborder. = Feliformia

6. Family. = Felidae

7. Subfamily. = Felinae

8. Genus. = Leopardus

9. Species. = Leopardus geoffroyi

10. Length. = 60 centimeters

11. Weight. = 5 kilogram

12. Speed. = 48 miles per hour

13. Geoffroy's cat are found in = Andes of southern Bolivia, Brazil, Paraguay, Argentina, Uruguay, Chile.

Geoffroy's cat

Geoffroy's cat (ज्योफ्रॉय बिल्ली)

The Geoffroy's cat is **about the size of a domestic cat**, but has numerous black spots and dark bands on the cheeks, head and neck as well as on the tail and limbs. The background colour of its fur varies from a brownish-yellow coat in the northern part of its range to a more grayish coat in the south. The Geoffroy's cat is mainly nocturnal, but does hunt at dawn and dusk. They like water and are keen swimmers. Geoffroy's cats are strong swimmers that regularly enter the water, and have been recorded frequently swimming fast flowing rivers.

Baby of Geoffroy's cat (Kitten)

Kitten (बिलौटा)

Geoffroy's cats are polygynous, which means that one male mates with multiple females. The male will mate with most of those females within his protected range. The mating season takes place from December to May. Gestation lasts for 67-78 days and females can produce one litter per year of one to four kittens. The mother gives birth inside a den which could be a rock crevice, bushes or a nook up in a tree. The kittens are born blind, their eyes opening within 8-12 days. The kittens develop quickly, being able to stand at around four days old, start to walk when two or three weeks old and climb fearlessly by six weeks.

Scientific classification of Andean Mountain cat

1. Kingdom. = Animalia

2. Phylum. = Chordata

3. Class. = Mammalia

4. Order. = Carnivora

5. Suborder. = Feliformia

6. Family. = Felidae

7. Sub family. = Felinae

8. Genus. = Leopardus

9. Species. = L.jacobita

10. Length. = 85 centimeters

11. Weight. = 8.1 kilogram

12. Andean Mountain cat are found in = Andes , Peru , Bolivia , Chile , Argentina.

Andean Mountain cat

Andean Mountain cat (एंडिएं पहाड़ी बिल्ली)

The Andean mountain cat is regarded as one of the world's most endangered wild cats and perhaps South America's rarest felid, yet, as far as cat species go, it is amongst the least known. It is a very rare animal, and its similarities with the more common South American Pampas cat have caused studying this species to be even more difficult. These cats have a similar size to domestic cats. However, their thick fur and their long tail make them look bigger. Their fur is ash-gray or pale silver and has isolated orange-brown or hazel stripes and spots. The cat's limbs and tail have black rings around them.

Baby of Andean Mountain cat (Kitten)

Kitten (बिलौटा)

Due to the very few observations in the wild, there are no records of the reproductive behavior of Andean mountain cats. By using the local people's observations of Andean mountain cats in pairs with their litters, the theory is arrived at that the Andean mountain cat's mating season is between July and August. Because some kittens are seen during April to October, the mating season may extend as far as November or December. A litter usually numbers one to three, born during spring or summer.

Scientific classification of Kodkod cat

1. Kingdom. = Animalia

2. Phylum. = Chordata

3. Class. = Mammalia

4. Order. = Carnivora

5. Suborder. = Feliformia

6. Family. = Felidae

7. Sub family. = Felinae

8. Genus. = Leopardus

9. Species. = Leoapardus

10. Length. = 51 centimeters

11. Weight. = 2 . 5 kilograms

12. Speed. = 30 miles per hour

13. Kodkod cat are found in = Chile , Argentina , America.

Kodkod cat

Kodkod cat (अमेरिका की छोटी बिल्लि)

The Kodkod is a secretive animal the size of a very small house cat, and along with the oncilla, is one of the southern hemisphere's smallest cats. It's tiny body has grayish-brown to buff fur, covered with many small black spots that will sometimes create broken streaks on its head and neck. The small head has low-set ears, black at the rear, with a central white spot. It's short tail is bushy and has narrow, black bands. It's rather large feet suggest it's ability to climb. Kodkod is the smallest wild cat in the Americas, found in Chil and Argentina.

It's scientific name is Leopardus guigna.

Baby of Kodkod cat (Kitten)

Kitten (बिलौटा)

The litter size of the female guignas range between one to four offspring , with a generation period of 72 to 78 days. There are also nominal data regarding parental investment in these felines. It is also through that the female teach the baby kodkods the hunting techniques before they become independent and are able to forage for themselves. Both the male and the female kittens attain the age of sexual maturity when they are about low years. There is no report about the mating season and breeding interval. As a behavior adaptation , guignas are excellent climbers , however , they do not seem to hunt it trees.

Scientific classification of Chinese Mountain cat

1. Kingdom. = Animalia

2. Phylum. = Chordata

3. Class. = Mammalia

4. Order. = Carnivora

5. Suborder. = Feliformia

6. Family. = Felidae

7. Sub family. = Felinae

8. Genus. = Felis

9. Species. = F.bieti

10. Length. = 78 centimeter

11. Weight. = 5.5 kilogram

12. Speed. = 30 miles per hour

13. Chinese Mountain cat are found in = China.

Chinese Mountain cat

Chinese Mountain cat (चीनी पहाड़ी बिल्ली)

The Chinese mountain cat is a small wild cat native to western China. It has sand-colored fur with dark guard hairs. Faint dark horizontal stripes on the face and legs are hardly visible. Its ears have black tips. It has a relatively broad skull and long hair growing between the pads of its feet. It is whitish on the belly, and its legs and tail bear black rings. Chinese mountain cat is found in China and lives on the north-eastern edge of the Tibetan Plateau. It was recorded only in eastern Qinghai and north-western Sichuan. It inhabits high-elevation steppe grassland, alpine meadow, alpine shrubland , and coniferous forest edges.

Baby of Chinese Mountain cat (Kitten)

Kitten (बिलौटा)

Chinese mountain cats have a polygynandrous (promiscuous) mating system in which both the males and the females have multiple partners. The breeding season takes place between January and March. After the gestation period of 60-75 days, females give birth to 2-4 kittens in a secluded burrow where they are safe from predators. The young are born blind and helpless. They grow quickly and become independent at age of 7 to 8 months. Reproductive maturity is usually reached between 8 and 12 months of age.

Scientific classification of Pampas cat

1. Kingdom. = Animalia

2. Phylum. = Chordata

3. Class. = Mammalia

4. Order. = Carnivora

5. Suborder. = Feliformia

6. Family. = Felidae

7. Sub family. = Felinae

8. Genus. = Leopardus

9. Species. = L. colocola

10. Length. = 60 centimeter

11. Weight. = 3 kilogram

12. Speed. = 30 miles per hour

13. Pampas cat are found in = Argentina , Chile , Patagonia , Savannah.

Pampas cat

Pampas cat (मैदान की बिल्ली)

Pampas cats look more **like heavier versions of domestic cats**. Their thick fur makes them look larger than they actually are. They have a broad face with a small muzzle and pointed ears. Their appearance is more similar to European wild cats than other South American cats. Leopardus colocolo, or generally called the pampas cats or just colocolo is a species of wild cats that is comparatively smaller in size than other wild cats with more resemblance to heavily built domestic cats. They show the most diversified choices of habitat among all South America cats.

Baby of Pampas cat (Kitten)

Kitten (बिलौटा)

The behavior and mating system of the Pampas cat are not known. In the northern hemisphere in captivity they breed from **April to July**. The gestation period is 80 to 85 days, with 1 to 3 being born per litter. The mother provides her young with milk. parental care are unknown, but, as with other cats, the young probably need caring for. They are likely born in a den and looked after by their mother until she takes them on foraging trips. In captivity, the young reach sexual maturity at about 21 months old.

9 789356 288577

Printed by Libri Plureos GmbH in Hamburg,
Germany